Communication Altern
in Autism

Communication Alternatives in Autism

Perspectives on Typing and Spelling
Approaches for the Nonspeaking

Edited by
EDLYN VALLEJO PEÑA

Toplight

Jefferson, North Carolina

LIBRARY OF CONGRESS CATALOGUING-IN-PUBLICATION DATA

Names: Peña, Edlyn Vallejo, 1979– editor.
Title: Communication alternatives in autism : perspectives on
typing and spelling approaches for the nonspeaking /
edited by Edlyn Vallejo Peña.
Description: Jefferson, North Carolina : Toplight, 2019 |
Includes bibliographical references and index.
Identifiers: LCCN 2019030812 | ISBN 9781476678917 (paperback) |
ISBN 9781476637136 (ebook) ∞
Subjects: LCSH: Communicative disorders in children. |
Nonverbal communication in children. | Children with
mental disabilities—Language.
Classification: LCC RJ496.C67 C64 2019 | DDC 618.92/855—dc23
LC record available at https://lccn.loc.gov/2019030812

BRITISH LIBRARY CATALOGUING DATA ARE AVAILABLE

ISBN (print) 978-1-4766-7891-7
ISBN (ebook) 978-1-4766-3713-6

Front cover images © 2019 Shutterstock

Printed in the United States of America

Toplight is an imprint of McFarland & Company, Inc., Publishers

*Box 611, Jefferson, North Carolina 28640
www.toplightbooks.com*

To my son
and brilliant teacher,
Diego

Table of Contents

Acknowledgments

First, thank you to the autistic co-authors, and the communication partners who supported them, for writing the powerful essays in *Communication Alternatives in Autism*. I am grateful for the time, effort, and passion you put forth. Tracy Thresher, Larry Bissonnette, Amy Sequenzia, Ido Kedar, Samuel Capozzi, Dillan Barmache, Henry Frost, Emma Zurcher-Long, Philip Reyes, and Rhema Russell—you are changing the world with your advocacy. I am honored you accepted my invitation to contribute to this collection.

I am forever grateful to my family and friends who supported me as I crafted this book with my co-authors. In particular, I am indebted to my loving husband, Dr. Damien Peña, and devoted mom, Maria Vallejo. Both of you have stood by me with unconditional love as you watched the creation of this book unfold from idea to finished product. I could not have done this without you two and son Diego Peña by my side.

Compensation to chapter authors would not have been made possible without financial contributions from California Lutheran University, the Graduate School of Education, and an anonymous donor. Thank you for awarding grants to fund author stipends for writing their chapters and sharing their wisdom.

This book underwent dozens of revisions. Each draft improved because of friends and colleagues who were willing to read and provide constructive feedback on particular areas of the manuscript. I appreciate your insights and attention to detail: Gita Gupta, Robin Mesaros, Amanda Johnson, Ali Steers, Dr. Nancy-Jean Pement, Seanon Jones-Kirsebom, Dr. Aja McKee, Dr. Casey Woodfield, Dr. Erin Ebersole, Dr. Mel Spence, Dr. Damien Peña, and Maria Vallejo.

Last but not least, I want to thank the village of people who have shaped my thinking about supporting people with disabilities, challenged my assumptions, and supported Diego Peña through his journey, both directly and indirectly: Amanda Johnson, Robin and Richard Mesaros, Soma Mukhopadhyay, Katie Anawalt, Lenae Crandall, Ali Steers, Elizabeth Vosseller, Natalie Dempsey, Dr. Lynn Koegel, Gerry Wurzburg, Pascal Cheng, Harvey Lavoy, Shelley Carnes, Kimberly Perry, Shamim Haldanker, the Capozzi family, Julie Sando Johnston, Dr. Mona Delahooke, Dr. Aimee Anderson, Dr. Kirsten Brown, Dr. Lissa Stapleton, Tauna Szymanski, and, last but not least, all of the families associated with the Autism and Communication Center at California Lutheran University.

Preface

Imagine, after decades of silence, discovering your voice without being able to speak. What would it mean to finally be heard by others after years of being dismissed, marginalized, and forgotten? Further, what would it mean to continue to be questioned for the kind of communication you have chosen and learned to use? *Communication Alternatives in Autism* explores the extraordinary first-hand journeys of people who confront issues of communication access, communication choice, as well as exclusion and inclusion in educational systems. To be clear, this book advocates for the consideration and use of methods that lead to communication in alternative ways—rapid prompting method and facilitated communication, in particular. These methods are regarded as highly controversial among particular autism professionals. At the same time, a number of medical doctors, psychologists, speech therapists, occupational therapists, teachers, and other support providers accept rapid prompting method and facilitated communication as legitimate forms of communication. At the heart of this book, at its very core, are the narratives of 10 autistic[1] self-advocates who actually use these methods to communicate. Their narratives document the complexities that autistic individuals navigate when choosing to use a highly controversial, alternative form of communication in educational and community settings. Using letter boards and keyboards to write their chapters, the authors describe powerful stories in the context of aiming for disability rights. Despite tremendous odds, each overcame systemic and personal obstacles, engaged in advocacy, and achieved triumph in accessing equitable opportunities in some form.

While this book is not intended to be used diagnostically, *Communication Alternatives in Autism* incorporates an analysis and discussion of research focused on the controversies, opportunities, and recommendations for those who use or wish to use rapid prompting method or facilitated communication. In the introduction, I review research and arguments made by professionals about the potential dangers and pitfalls of the teaching methods behind using letter boards and keyboards to communicate. I situate my personal experiences as a parent of Diego, a nonspeaking child with autism, in the context of this controversy. The introduction emphasizes what Diego so articulately points out—"It is my right as a person to always have communication no matter how controversial it is."

The chapters that follow are written by autistic self-advocates and are organized into three sections. In the first section of essays, "Escaping the Institutionalization Mindset," Tracy Thresher, Larry Bissonnette, and Amy Sequenzia—all of whom were born at a time when autistic children were institutionalized—document the inequitable opportunities to communicate afforded to them at that time. They each describe the ways in which they achieved access to communication in their adult years, a turning point in their lives that enabled them to become self-advocates. By contrast, the second section of essays, "A Movement Toward Full Inclusion," written by Ido Kedar, Samuel Capozzi, and Dillan Barmache, reflect the experiences of a generation of autistics who gained access to full educational inclusion by the time they reached high school and college. Ido, Samuel, and Dillan make important recommendations to educators and caregivers that underscore possibilities and opportunities for future generations of minimally-speaking and nonspeaking students. In the third section of essays, "Triumphs and Obstacles in Navigating the Educational Maze," Henry Frost, Emma Zurcher-Long, Philip Reyes, and Rhema Russell provide an inside view into the experiences of young people with autism who represent a range of schooling experiences. On the one hand, the narratives included in the second and third sections reveal a more positive shift in access to communication choice and opportunities in recent years. On the other, the authors articulate the many challenges and obstacles they continue to endure and overcome with regard to inclusion in school systems.

The appendix concludes this work by presenting research-based educational practices that schools and colleges enact to support students who use alternative forms of communication. These promising practices are grounded in the results of a qualitative interview study of 14 educators and communication partners across the United States who successfully support students who use letter boards and keyboards to communicate. The concluding chapter includes practical recommendations regarding developing foundational beliefs about students with autism, opportunities for access to communication, and opportunities for participation and engagement in educational environments. These three major themes emerged across the chapter narratives in combination with the results of the qualitative interview study. The framework of recommendations will equip educators, therapists, and the larger autism community who aim to improve inclusion and communication rights for autistic individuals.

Altogether, this book weaves together narratives of people with autism, original research, and my own personal experiences as a parent. By combining qualitative narratives of autistic self-advocates with research findings, it not only offers a unique and rich resource to autistics, family members, educators, and therapists, it also contributes to scholarly conversations about the power of access to communication, inclusion, and possibility for people with autism. Ultimately my co-authors and I desire to give other people with autism and limited speech a fighting chance at accessing communication. Further, we support increased representation and meaningful, legitimate participation of autistics at all levels of society since, historically, they have been silenced by others. In other words, we advocate for a life filled with meaning and purpose for all people with autism who require alternative forms of communication.

It is important to note that I myself am not a person with autism, and therefore never claim to be an autism expert. I use my position of privilege as an academic scholar to make a research-based case alongside my autistic co-authors to support the needs and interests of autistic people with complex communication differences. The richness and true spirit of the book lies in the chapters written by the 10 autistic individuals who live and breathe the autism experience. As the editor of the book, I took great care to offer helpful feedback to contributors as they developed their narratives without compromising their personal writing style, voice, and message. Each essay is unique. All together, they reflect a cross-section of the authors' personalities, sense-making, ages, access to resources, and educational experiences. I am forever grateful for their effort and courage in contributing their personal stories to *Communication Alternatives in Autism*. Yes, they are the true autism experts. Their narrative accounts will challenge you to reconsider society's deep-seated assumptions about the capabilities of people with autism, never leaving you the same.

NOTE

1. The terms autistic and person with autism are used interchangeably in this book to honor the varying preferences of how people on the spectrum, including the chapter authors, wish to identify.

Introduction:
From Confession to Declaration

Edlyn Vallejo Peña, Ph.D.

Five years ago, my husband and I confessed to our five-year old autistic son's teacher, speech therapist, and behavioral therapy team that he used an alternative form of communication for people with autism that remains highly contested. The innocuous sounding approach involves pointing to letters on a laminated letter board (also called an alphabet board) or a keyboard to communicate. Letter by letter, individuals who have limited means of speaking use this mode of communication to spell and type their thoughts. Yet the stakes are high when a confession about this kind of communication is made. Given some of the prevailing perspectives in the field of autism, an admission like ours could be used against our son or any individual who communicates in this way. A confession such as the one we shared with our son's educational team could mean the difference between being granted or denied access to his preferred method of communication. But how could any form of communication for a nonspeaking person possibly be considered controversial, and in some professional circles, even condemned and banned? Pointing to letters or typing on a keyboard must be harmless, right?

Our son, Diego, learned to communicate on a letter board and keyboard using the highly-critiqued approach called Rapid Prompting Method (RPM). The vehement opposition to Diego's communication by a few teachers and behavioral therapists was based on a number of researchers and practitioners who declared RPM to be a discredited

form of authentic communication, suggesting the communication partner or facilitator effectively influences the message generated. Our deepest fear for Diego was that, without access to a letter board and a trained
communication partner at his side, he would not be able to keep up
with his peers in a general education classroom, eventually forcing him
to be placed in a segregated special education class. Diego's journey is
not unique. Other autistic students in the United States and around the
world have found themselves in this precarious position. They communicate fluently with letter boards or keyboards at home, yet are barred
from doing so in schools. For this reason, students and their families
continue to lose the fight to choose their preferred mode of communication in public school settings when that choice is RPM. Families have
learned the hard way that educators and service providers, when
opposed to RPM, have the power to provide or deny access to vital
resources. Such resources include therapy, assistive technology, and
therefore inclusion, in schooling and community experiences. This
became our reality when one teacher's protests during first grade put
Diego in jeopardy of losing the primary method with which he communicated at school.

Do you understand now why this kind of confession becomes carefully guarded? As a parent, you become a protector of this kind of delicate information, vigilant about how and to whom you share. You only
confess to things in private spaces at first. "I have a secret," you might
say. Then slowly, you admit to friends who are generally open to new
possibilities. "What I'm about to tell you is controversial," you might
share in a hushed tone. Feeling emboldened by supportive responses,
you confess to strangers when you begin to feel brave. "My son/daugh-
ter/client/student types to communicate," you might declare. Your emer-
gent courage begins to take root. You reassure yourself that you have
made the right decision to support this individual's form of communication whole-heartedly. I understand first-hand the layers of courage
that are peeled away as you grow more confident, knowing that the way
in which your son/daughter/client/student communicates is something
to be shared unapologetically. The transition from quiet confession to
unrestrained declaration is a journey that requires audacity in the face
of skeptics.

The reality is that the community of autistic people who use letter boards and keyboards to communicate is growing worldwide (see, for example, Deacy, Jennings, & O'Halloran, 2016). As an historically marginalized group, autistics who experience complex communication differences are increasing their demands of inclusion and communication supports. Thanks to narratives published in books and posted on the internet (e.g., https://unitedforcommunicationchoice.org), their voices, their typed words, are being heard and read. People in all spheres are beginning to pay attention to what autistics have to say about their experiences. In turn, we are beginning to legitimize the teaching methods employed to enable students to use letter boards and keyboards as alternative communication strategies. To provide some context for the premise of this book, let me begin by telling you more about a little boy who changed my life, and changed my ideas about what it means to have a voice.

French Fries and Jelly Beans

From the day Diego arrived home from the hospital in 2008, he spent his first five years of life growing up in a quaint condominium bordering the campus of California State University, Channel Islands in southern California. The university had been converted into a postsecondary campus after its decades-long run as the notorious Camarillo State Hospital. Since 1936, the hospital was otherwise known as a "mental institution" for people with disabilities, including autism. Just 11 years before Diego's birth, the hospital closed its doors for the last time. By then, autistic children were beginning to be offered more humane, ethical, and inclusive therapies.

Not long after Diego's second birthday, he was diagnosed with autism. I wondered, had Diego been born just over one decade earlier, would he have been institutionalized? Would he have been put away, a victim of forced isolation and questionable human experiments? His fate, it seemed, was largely determined by the timing of his birth. Rather than growing up behind the white walls of the institution, where in some cases electro-shock therapy and lobotomies occurred, Diego played on the fields of a postsecondary campus which enrolled and supported students with disabilities. Hope and opportunity bloomed.

In the early years of Diego's behavioral and speech therapy, his speech development was painfully slow. Countless hours of therapy—often involving restricted access to favorite foods or activities until he completed a task—left Diego in tears, banging his small fists against the sofa. The tasks, for a child like Diego, were no walk in the park. Much of the programming was focused on teaching Diego compliance through repeated discrete trials and rote instruction. Imagine being asked to touch the right color over and over when your body does not cooperate with you, when you experience motor problems, or when your sensory issues are amplified. After countless months of this kind of behavioral therapy, Diego began to shut down, unresponsive to his therapists' bids for attention. I'd had enough. The twinkle in his eye was fading, a sign the daily behavioral therapy sessions were slowly chipping away at his spirit.

It just so happened that the very first iPad was released several months after Diego's second birthday. When traditional speech and behavioral therapy failed, I began researching other options for therapeutic approaches to assist Diego with his communication. I came upon augmentative and alternative communication (AAC). AAC involves communicating by means other than oral speech. Gestures, symbols, pictures, and words can be used within the context of augmentative aids, such as electronic devices and laminated communication boards. When a person has a difficult time speaking, AAC can mean the difference between getting one's basic needs met, or not. Sadly, not all of Diego's therapists believed in the power of AAC. "He's too young," they explained, "to give up on traditional speech therapy." The behavioral therapists held the erroneous assumption that AAC would inhibit his speech development, even though no evidence existed to support that premise (Millar, Light & Schlosser, 2006; Blischak, Lombardino & Dyson, 2003). Further, our local public school declined to provide supports with using his iPad as a communication device when Diego turned three. After a 20-minute assistive technology assessment, the school speech therapist concluded he was "not ready" to use such an AAC device. She explained that Diego was only capable of using the iPad as a toy rather than for functional communication.

My gut instinct told me not to listen. After all, you can't introduce a child to a swimming pool for the first time and expect him to swim after a 20-minute assessment. I believed Diego would be ready if he was simply taught to use an iPad with a proper communication app as a communication device. Not a radical concept; but perhaps it was radical for a speech pathologist who didn't believe in a nonspeaking child's capabilities. Instead, I thought, let's teach this kid to communicate! After quite a bit of cajoling on my end, the behavioral therapists on Diego's team agreed to teach Diego to use a symbol-based communication app on a dedicated iPad. My hope for Diego began to restore. Within a few months, Diego reliably asked for his favorite foods and activities. A month later, I added the symbol for "hug" in his iPad. On that day, Diego brought me his iPad and told me "I want hug." His small hand grasped mine and led me to the couch to snuggle. It was the most meaningful communicative moment I had with Diego in his 3.5 years. For the first time, Diego used "words" to connect with me, strengthening our relationship as mother and son.

By using the symbol-based communication app, Diego began communicating in more meaningful ways between the ages of three and four. He hit the "french fries" symbol before I had the chance to order food when we went through a fast food restaurant drive-thru. You bet that I honored his request! He pressed the "quiet" symbol, demanding his father and I lower our voices while he watched his favorite cartoon. We chuckled and began to whisper.

Still, we found that the pre-programmed symbols limited Diego's ability to express himself beyond the symbols that were available on the app. By the time Diego reached the age of four, he experimented with creative ways to request items and express himself. He wanted jellybeans at school, but no symbol with a jellybean was programmed into his app. Diego carefully searched through the symbols. He selected an egg icon, mimicking the shape of the jellybean. Clever. When Diego asked for the video of "It's the Great Pumpkin, Charlie Brown" he was again at a disadvantage. No Charlie Brown symbol existed. He navigated through the app into the folder of symbols with colors and pushed "brown." Resourceful.

Even more, we discovered Diego's potential to communicate by spelling. Diego's preschool aide, Natalie, texted me one day to say, "I forgot to tell you Diego spelled 'ladybug' by himself at the science table on Thursday. It was pretty awesome." Diego had accessed the letter symbols on his iPad communication app. I wondered what other thoughts were in his head that sought to be given a voice. What else would Diego have to say if he could type out his thoughts? I longed to discover Diego's feelings, his thoughts, his personality. I knew he had the capacity to spell words in contextually-relevant situations. I just didn't know how to tap into his ability to spell out his thoughts.

Bring on the Letter Board!

In an eager search for answers, I spent days and nights scouring the internet and research journals for ideas, therapeutic approaches, and educational strategies to enhance Diego's communication. I initially took the traditional route, consulting with "autism experts" who had Ph.D.s and M.D.s. However, the answers there were limited. I became increasingly intrigued by learning from autistic individuals themselves. I yearned to know, from their perspective, what it was like to be autistic. In late 2012, I happened upon a book called *Ido in Autismland* (2012), written by an autistic young man who uses a letter board to communicate. That book changed the trajectory of my journey to support Diego. With each page I turned, Ido disrupted my misguided notions that lack of speech equates to lack of intelligence; that students with autism are incapable of expressing or recognizing emotions; and that all students who are non-speaking belong in special day classes without the opportunity for inclusion. Contrary to many of the messages the world receives on a daily basis about people with autism, Ido's book informs us that the minds of people with autism are as complex, creative, and intelligent as yours and mine. On a personal level, reading Ido's book was transformative and allowed my relationship with my son to turn a corner. I began to talk to Diego like I would any other smart and capable child. I made efforts to talk *to* Diego, not *about* him, when he was in the room.

Not too long after reading *Ido in Autismland*, I met an extraordinary young man named Samuel Capozzi. Samuel was 17 years old and had just learned to communicate using RPM the year prior. I met with Samuel and his parents to take them on a tour of the university where I teach and work. When we sat down to chat, Samuel asked me on his letter board, "You really believe I can go to college, don't you?" I didn't hesitate, "Absolutely, without a doubt!" This conversation gave me hope, not only for Samuel, but for Diego and other young people like him. They all had the right to a quality education no matter what kind of communication they used. The combination of reading Ido's compelling book and looking into Samuel's hopeful eyes spurred me to introduce Diego to professionals, including the RPM founder Soma Mukhopadhyay, who taught him to use the letter board and keyboard to communicate.

As Diego learned to communicate over many months between the ages of five and six, my husband and I began to peel away the layers of our son's personality and character. He typed messages that often reflected complex ideas. Not, "My favorite color is blue," kind of thoughts. More like, "[I am a] Free Spirit. Peaceful. Reasonable," at the age of six years old. He requested to learn about the history of peace and the biography of the Dalai Lama. He also revealed his humorous side to persuade us to fulfill his dreams: "I am hearing going to [an] Hawaii escape teaches bright typing." Four years later, we fulfilled his request by visiting the shores of Oahu.

The summer in between Diego's kindergarten and first grade years, we practiced communicating with the letter board until he was fairly proficient at answering open-ended questions. The week before Diego started first grade, Diego's therapist, who had been trained in RPM, asked him what he anticipated from going back to school. He typed, "Total chaos." Little did we know his premonition was absolutely on point. After observing Diego and his aide using the letter board in the classroom, one of his teachers questioned whether his aide was typing or influencing the messages generated by Diego. It was suspicious to her that Diego used "big words" like "justice," she told us, and that he wrote about how supportive his aide was a number of times. It must have been the aide feeding Diego these words, they believed. After all, Diego did not respond or spell responses with such sophistication when his new teachers held the letter board. The teachers interpreted his difficulty with generalizing his communication skills across communication partners as a sign that his responses were fabricated by his aide. The teacher demanded that the aide stop holding the letter board, which is a necessary practice in RPM before the student is able to independently spell or type with the letter board on a table or stand. The teacher's decision interrupted Diego's ability to produce original, open-ended thoughts, hampering his ability to participate fully in classroom discussions.

In addition to denied access to his primary mode of communication at school, we experienced denied access to RPM at home with our applied behavior analysis therapy team. The supervisor of the team adamantly refused to provide behavioral therapy to Diego if we persisted in using RPM to teach Diego to use his letter board for communication. RPM is not an evidenced-based practice, he argued. While trying to make sense of the oppositional responses Diego received from educators and therapists, I came across a blog, "Emma's Hope Book." Emma, a young woman who types to communicate, and a contributor to this essay collection, had gone through similar struggles with her school. Her mother, Ariane, wrote: "The discrepancy between what they witnessed (watching Emma type) and what they had been trained to believe was, for a great many, too vast. And even those who truly believed Emma was competent, they had no idea how to bridge what they'd been trained to do and teach, and what they saw her capable of learning with RPM."

My husband and I decided there was absolutely nothing Diego's teacher or behavioral supervisor could say to change our minds about Diego's communication. We couldn't "unsee" what Diego showed us as he spelled message upon message. My husband and I agreed to part ways with the behavioral company on the principle that nothing was more important than giving Diego access to communication. And after several months of feuding with Diego's teacher, the district transitioned him to a new school in the middle of the academic year. This teacher, a single individual, decided Diego's fate—forcing him to change schools, become acquainted with a new teacher and classroom dynamics, and begin new friendships with unfamiliar peers. Diego lamented that his teacher had "killed my spirit." During this dark period in our family's life, we reached deep down inside of ourselves to muster our strength, courage, and resilience. We considered ourselves blessed that we hadn't endured multiple changes in therapy companies and schools like other students had. Still, the fight for Diego's educational inclusion and access to communication was difficult beyond measure, but nonetheless worthwhile.

Controversial Communication

All the autistic authors in this book learned to communicate using RPM or another method that encourages communication on a keyboard called facilitated communication (FC). In RPM, the communication partner holds an alphabet stencil, a laminated letter board, or wireless keyboard while verbally prompting the communicator to spell or type responses. The verbal prompts provide instruction, encouragement, and guidance with motor planning to point to the next letter. The communication partner eventually fades prompts, including holding the letter board and keyboard. This occurs as the communicator and communication partner build their skills from predictable answers to open-ended responses that are unpredictable to the communication partner. In FC, an entirely different method, the facilitator uses physical support at the wrist, forearm, elbow, or shoulder with the goal of fading that physical support once the communicator becomes proficient at communicating on the keyboard (Ashby & Kasa, 2013). FC can also be used to support someone to point to pictures, symbols, and words. Individuals who use FC have motor and movement difficulties which affect their ability to point independently or reliably when using communication aids or devices. The physical support provided helps individuals to improve their pointing skills so that they can use these aids and devices more effectively. In addition, verbal prompts aim to provide emotional encouragement and feedback to communicators as they build their communicative proficiency and independence. The common goal for both RPM and FC is to eventually develop independent communication skills by fading prompts, eliminating the need for a facilitator to physically support or hold a letter board or keyboard for the communicator. Achieving this level of independence is difficult but possible through proper training for both the communicator and the communication partner (Ashby & Kasa, 2013; Cardinal & Falvey, 2014).

The debate about whether FC and RPM are valid forms of communication is as heated as any political dispute. The chief question defining this controversy is: Who is the author of the message being typed? Is it the facilitator (also called a communication partner)? Or is it the student? The answers to these questions can be traced back to the early 1990s. Experimental studies conducted during that time reported damning results: typed responses using FC methods were either influenced by the facilitator or participants were not able to successfully pass messages. During message-passing tasks, explained Rossetti, Cheng, & Lavoy (2012),

> The communicator communicates information which is unknown to their facilitator. This response could be in the form of pointing to a picture, symbol, or word or typing a word, phrase, or statement of which the facilitator is unaware. The ability to accurately convey information under these conditions demonstrates that the communicator is the author of their communication and can provide examples of the validity of their communication over time [p. 4].

Message passing was tested under double blind study conditions where the facilitator and communicator did not know whether they were seeing the same image or different images. The results under message-passing experiments showed that the communicator usually answered the question wrong when given physical support by the facilitator. When facilitators were blind to the information being presented, the communicators were not able to provide accurate responses. The conclusion: the facilitator unconsciously influenced the communicator's message.

Opponents of FC and RPM argue there are dangerous consequences when a facilitator influences the communication output of their students or clients, whether consciously or unconsciously. Simply influencing the answer to a question like, "What is your favorite topic in school?" is seemingly innocuous. But several cases have surfaced in the media in which students who used FC have falsely communicated that a parent has sexually abused them. These cases resulted in emotional and legal turmoil. Parents were temporarily jailed and children were removed from their homes for months. Without question, such examples are horrific, leaving families unnecessarily broken and traumatized.

If FC has been seemingly discredited by numerous experimental studies, and in some cases resulted in false accusations, why continue this conversation? After all, national organizations such as the American Speech-language Hearing Association have publicly condemned FC and RPM (ASHA, 2018). First, while false statements have been produced through these controversial methods, on the one hand, important information produced by FC and RPM users have also been confirmed as true, on the other. For instance, as early as 1994, researchers analyzed the medical records of over 1,000 children who reported sexual abuse in upstate

New York from 1990–1993 (Botash et al.). Among these records, 13 cases of sexual abuse were reported by children using FC, either to a facilitator or teacher. After further medical and legal investigations into the 13 cases,

> seven children… were determined to be indicative of abuse by CPS. The indication rate for abuse and neglect in this series is consistent with the upstate New York indication rate of approximately 47%. These results demonstrate that allegations of abuse that are initiated owing to an FC disclosure should be taken seriously [p. 1287].

Further, parents and professionals have reported instances in which their child complained of pain or discomfort in particular areas of their body through RPM and FC methods. Such complaints were medically validated by doctors after investigating the child's symptoms. General practitioners, neurologists, and pediatricians have issued medical diagnoses after listening to the complaints of individuals who type and spell to communicate. In particular, parents and professionals have shared in online groups that symptoms described by RPM and FC users have resulted in diagnoses of seizures, impacted wisdom teeth and cavities, kidney stones, heart conditions, urinary tract infections, gastrointestinal problems, and food allergies (personal communication, November 23, 2018). In a more poignant example, a 49 year-old man who had learned to communicate using RPM reportedly spelled out, "Stop. I am in need of medical attention" (https://juniperhillfarms.org, 2018). After describing his symptoms, his doctor discovered he had testicular cancer. Not only did the doctor treat the cancer, but the man is now cancer free. I had the privilege to meet him in person one year after receiving a clean bill of health from his oncologist. His account compels me to ask: What might this man's fate be had he been relegated to silence and not had access to RPM to communicate his urgent medical condition?

Based on the spectrum of accounts about the authenticity of messages produced by FC and RPM users, two inferences can be made. First, methods that include a communication partner or facilitator can be subject to influence. In fact, virtually all methods that teach augmentative and alternative communication to minimally speaking people require a support person, communication partner, or interventionist. If allegations are made about abuse, additional steps and safeguards should be taken when investigating such allegations. Under these circumstances, individuals may turn to resources such as "Guidelines for Handling Allegations of Abuse While Using Facilitated Communication," a report produced by the Developmental Disability Services Division of Vermont (2018). Second, not all communication output that involves a communication partner or facilitator is influenced or harmful. The risk of influence must be mitigated through supervised practice and continued research on improving the quality, rigor, and fidelity of the methods. Further, it is worth noting that the complexity and depth of communication produced by the communicator is contingent on the kind of communication offered by the partner or interventionist, regardless of what the communicator actually desires to express. As Larry Bissonnette wisely concludes in his conference presentations, "Operating pictures on a board brings you a cheeseburger. Typing lets you create the menu."

A Call for More Research

Important questions about facilitated communication (FC) and rapid prompting method (RPM) certainly remain unanswered. For instance, we have little understanding about whether a relationship exists between the accuracy of message passing and the amount of physical support or prompting given by the communication partner. Some communicators who use FC only require a hand placed on the communicator's knee or back. Other individuals who learned to communicate using RPM can type or spell with the keyboard in the stand without being held by the communication partner. Is the message produced in these instances more likely to be correct in a message-passing experiment? In addition, communicators and facilitators have different levels of training and experience, both independently and with one another. At the time of the studies conducted in the 1990s, systematic methods for FC training and rigor were not yet established. Does the nature and quality of the communicator and facilitators' training impact the accuracy of the message? The conditions of the experiments and intentions of the researcher may have also played a role in the studies' outcomes. Is there an impact on communicators knowing that many of the studies were designed by researchers who questioned the validity of their communication, and therefore, their competence? Lastly, critics question why typed responses are successfully produced with only one or a few communication partners, usually individuals who have developed a relationship and practiced with the communicator. Generalization of skills is certainly difficult for people with autism across different settings and contexts. Why are individuals able to communicate fluently with one communication partner, but not a brand new one? To be sure, plenty of other unanswered questions exist and require exploration.

While facilitator influence can be a real issue in FC and RPM, evidence continues to emerge that communicators can demonstrate trustworthy authorship of their messages. The Committee on Educational Interventions for Students with Autism, supported by the United States National Research Council (2001), issued a report determining that even though "quantitative studies reveal no validation for FC, there are several qualitative studies indicating that some children with autism have developed independent communication skills through training in FC" (p. 62). The documentation of individuals who achieved independence in their typing suggests the potential for trustworthy authorship can be achievable. One study, Bigozzi, Zanobini, Tarchi, Cozzani, & Camba (2012), involved a group of six autistic boys who used FC to communicate. All participants were considered more advanced and independent in their communication, having used FC for at least five years and requiring support at the shoulder or other part of the body. None of the participants were physically supported at the hand, wrist, or arm. The analysis of the interactions between student and communication partner were done within the context of natural conversation. While the study did not follow experimental design procedures, considered a gold standard among many researchers, the findings of this study point to interactions that suggest authentic authorship. These included times when students asked for clarification from facilitator, when students' facial expressions or giggles matched the message they typed, or when students staunchly disagreed with the communication partner. Video clips of independent communicators can be found on the United for Communication Choice website at www.unitedforcommunicationchoice.org under "Videos of Advanced Learners." You will see compelling examples of students who type independently on an iPad or other communication device while the parent sits nearby and provides verbal encouragement to continue typing or spelling.

While FC has undergone a number of studies, RPM is, without question, under-researched (Deacy, Jennings, & O'Halloran, 2016). Those opposed to FC often view RPM as a form of FC, even though the methods are vastly distinct in their origins and techniques. RPM is branded as an educational method that eventually leads to communication. The communication partner encourages the communicator without physical support, usually in the form of holding an alphabet stencil, letter board, or keyboard in front of the communicator, using verbal prompts, and engaging the student with gestural prompts. Only a few studies on RPM exist. The most informative is a published case report conducted by occupational therapists that described improvements in engagement, communication, and participation in the context of daily activities for an autistic young man (McQuiddy & Brennan, 2016). To many researchers, this case study does not provide sufficient evidence to answer the question of communicator authenticity but it stands as a rare account of RPM in a research journal.

The call for more research on FC and RPM must not limit its focus on the question of authorship. Nonspeaking and minimally-speaking autistic individuals contend with a number of underlying challenges and symptoms that play a role in the dynamics of communicating on keyboards and letter boards. Research must continue to uncover answers to sensory differences, motor planning differences, and anxiety, all of which have been documented to some extent in the autism literature. The relationship among these experiences and alternative communication is not yet well understood. Doing so requires researchers and practitioners to consider multiple sources of data (e.g., interviews, narratives, field notes) to give us a more holistic picture beyond what can be revealed through quantitative methods within the context of experimental studies. Engaging in research studies to address unanswered questions will help the autism community determine the conditions under which FC and RPM, when done ethically and with rigor, can be successful. Further, the answers to these questions will enable the FC and RPM communities to move past the question of authorship toward addressing sensory, motor, and anxiety challenges that impact communication as well as improving training of communicators and facilitators. Rather than determining that a form of communication which is subject to influence is therefore dangerous and should thus be stopped, professionals should be committed to understanding ways in which to reduce influence and to support the progressive independence and reliability of the communicator.

I often ask myself, what if I or another communication partner is influencing Diego's typed responses? While we are careful not to influence his messages, even if subconsciously, it is a real possibility. After all, communication between two neurotypical individuals involves a dynamic exchange of words colored by expressions and emotions. Communication is not enacted independently. To say that traditional conversations do not involve influence from one communicator to another is unrealistic. In the case of RPM and FC, we cannot expect communicative exchanges to be sterile, but it is still wise to be vigilant about unintentional influence. No one wants to see the communicator express themselves in an authentic manner more than the communicator themselves.

Meanwhile, I cannot ignore the moments when what Diego typed or spelled was completely accurate and impossible for his communication partner to know. I remember the time in first grade when he told us he had an earache in his left ear. A visit to the pediatrician's office confirmed he had an ear infection. Or the time Diego wrote a silly poem during a first-grade assignment about smelling his grandmother's toes as she lay down in bed. "As grandma day dreams, I sneak. Smell her toes. Grandma not mad." His grandmother, with some embarrassment and humor, confirmed that detail. Or the time Diego self-identified as "Mexi-Cuban," the label that was lovingly given to him by his Dad to showcase his mixed heritage. Diego's communication partner had not heard this term before he typed it. In addition, he learned to communicate across five different communication partners in a given period of time. How could all five of his partners possibly get him to say witty and snarky remarks, reflecting his personality with such consistency? Diego's voice was his, regardless of who was holding the letter board.

These are but a few examples that authentic messages can be produced by individuals who have learned to communicate via RPM or FC. Despite hearing from a few autism professionals that Diego's communication was not trustworthy, I clung to the instances when he produced messages that were undeniably his. In these moments, I did not question that the words Diego spelled and communicated reflected his authentic voice. My commitment to his communication fortifies when I observe other autistic individuals who type on keyboards without touch or the keyboard being held. Although they require their communication partner at their side or somewhere near them—likely for emotional and sensory regulation support—they independently type each letter, word, and sentence. With practice, Diego will achieve this level of independence. In the meantime, I will not deny him his voice. The answer is to continue seeking support to practice FC or RPM with rigor, fidelity, and ethics. Along these lines, a report by the National Research Council (2001) makes recommendations for researchers and practitioners, encouraging them to keep searching for answers: "Past research that invalidates FC should not preempt research and practice in keyboarding, literacy learning, and AAC as a communication modality for children with autistic spectrum disorders." Rather, the report concluded, "it draws attention to the need for continued evaluation of independence and functional value in using new techniques" (p. 62). As such, more research is needed and autism service providers are encouraged to continue experimenting with methods that provide access to communication.

Underestimated Abilities

I am compelled to acknowledge the pervasive assumptions which reinforce conclusions that autistic individuals with limited speech could not possibly be authoring their own messages. Limited speech refers to the experience of being nonspeaking, minimally speaking, or having unreliable speech that is incongruent with one's own thoughts. The historically prevailing paradigm among autism professionals is that nonspeaking, minimally speaking, and unreliably speaking equals non-thinking. In fact, the underestimation of abilities runs rampant for students with disabilities in the education system. A report published by the National Center on Education Outcomes (NCEO) estimates that "the vast majority of special education students (80–85 percent) can meet the same achievement standards as other students if they are given specially designed instruction, appropriate access, supports and accommodations as required by federal law" (Thurlow, Quenemoen, & Lazarus, 2011, p. 5). The aftermath of a system operating under a deficit framework of disability results in inequitable opportunities and outcomes for students with disabilities.

The assumption that nonspeaking equals non-thinking undoubtedly affects the interpretation of the observations and conclusions made about FC and RPM. Reframing the deeply entrenched idea that minimally speaking individuals are also intellectually disabled is a monumental effort. For one, doing so undermines decades of research that children with "nonverbal autism" are not intellectually intact. Put another way, the notion that nonspeaking children are intelligent and capable of language directly contradicts much of their theory and practice. A major issue is that achievement and intelligence assessments are limited in their capacity to precisely measure the cognitive ability of a student with limited speech. First, researchers are often not able to administer cognitive testing to "minimally verbal" individuals because such tests rely on speech. When tests are administered to these individuals, they achieve low scores despite demonstrating evidence of cognitive skills in other contexts. Consequently, language impairment is viewed as synonymous with cognitive impairment, and autistic children who are minimally verbal are often referred to as low functioning or excluded from research studies altogether (Bal, Katz, Bishop, & Krasileva, 2016).

Evidence continues to mount that autistic students are often underestimated by way of intelligence testing. In 2016, a team of medical researchers published one of the largest studies of so-called "minimally verbal" students (Bal et al., 2016, p. 1424). The results of the study challenge the widespread assumption that autistic students who have difficulty with speech must have low intelligence. In a sample of 1,470 minimally verbal autistic children, researchers found that 43 to 52 percent of participants scored higher on their nonverbal scores compared to their verbal scores. In contrast, participants without disabilities achieved similar scores on both parts of the intelligence tests. In yet another study, Soulières and her colleagues administered alternative assessments to 30 minimally verbal children that focused on "autistic cognitive strengths" using "strength-informed assessments" rather than conventional instruments (Courchesne, Meilleur, Poulin-Lord, Dawson, & Soulières, 2016, p. 1). While none of the children in the study could complete the conventional instrument to measure intelligence, at least 26 of the children were able to complete one or more alternative assessments. On one of the assessment instruments, autistic children actually out-performed typically developing children. Their conclusion? Minimally verbal autistic children run the risk of being underestimated and "wrongly regarded as having little cognitive potential" (p. 1).

The findings that minimally speaking students are underestimated suggest language difficulties do not necessarily stem from cognitive problems in children with autism. Rather, the researchers suggest that language difficulties in some children are related to challenges associated with motor planning, such as "impaired imitation skills ... [and] oral-motor dysfunction" (Bal, Katz, Bishop, & Krasileva, 2016, p. 1431). Nearly 80 percent of students with autism experience some sort of motor impairment (Green, et al., 2009), reflecting challenges in sequencing of motor patterns (Cattaneo, et al., 2007). Activities that most people take for granted—tying shoelaces, writing with a pencil, getting dressed in the morning—can be excruciatingly difficult and frustrating for autistic individuals with uncooperative bodies. However, historically, researchers and clinicians in behavioral and medical fields have not considered motor problems in their treatment of people with autism. Rather, they interpreted a person's inability to complete tasks, including those required on intelligence tests, as cognitive impairments rather than motor impairments. The consequences of this interpretation directly affect the educational and therapeutic interventions afforded to autistic individuals:

> The conventional view is that most individuals with autism or pervasive developmental disorder-not otherwise specified (PDD-NOS) have no significant motor impairments but do have severe intellectual disabilities. These assumptions impact the nature and types of augmentative and alternative communication (AAC) interventions that are typically provided, which tend to be narrowly focused on basic, functional communication skills such as requesting [Mirenda, 2008, p. 220].

Donnellan, Hill, and Leary (2010; 2013) have extensively documented sensory and movement differences, described as "difficulties in starting, stopping, continuing, combining and switching motor action, speech, thought, memory and emotion" (Donnellan, Hill, & Leary, 2010, p. 1). These sensory and movement differences, Donnellan and her colleagues argue, are significant and go unrecognized far too often. Unlike other medical disorders such as Parkinson's, Tourette's, and Obsessive Compulsive Disorder, where movement differences are deemed as involuntary, professionals have historically regarded movement differences in autistic individuals as voluntary. Consequently, these "autistic behaviors" and actions are attributed to social and behavioral problems. However, there is a fundamental problem with this conclusion:

> Many of us have accepted without question the implicit message that unusual movements presented by people with autism are always volitional and often pleasurable.... Neurological symptoms, such as sudden, loud vocalizations;

being in constant motion; extreme response to minor changes; unusual man-nerisms and gait; and "unmotivated" laughter are examples of behaviors commonly thought to be performed "on purpose" and targeted for behavioral intervention. A social interpretation of these symptoms leaves people with the assumption that they occur as a matter of choice, apathy, or learned behavior [Donnellan et al., 2013, p. 6].

Movement differences, including repetitive motor actions such as tap-ping and rocking, and lack of initiation are not only attributed to non-compliance and apathy, but also to cognitive impairment and intellectual disability (Donnellan, Leary, & Robledo, 2006).

The consequences to misguided assumptions and faulty interpre-tations of intelligence test scores are very real and potentially damaging. Scores from intelligence testing can (mis)inform a diagnosis, placement in special education, and access to supports and services. Test results can also determine the extent to which teachers and therapists engage the student in instruction. An autistic student who lacks coordination and experiences sensory integration issues is likely to be labeled as non-compliant, lazy, slow, and intellectually disabled. The autistic student bears the double burden of being both misunderstood and blamed for a body over which s/he has little control. Worse, the student is excluded from social and educational opportunities. "Differences in the way peo-ple are able to use their bodies and focus their attention leads many to assume that a person does not care to participate or communicate and does not desire relationships," state Donnellan and her colleagues. "These assumptions affect our expectations, the way we speak with them and the educational and social opportunities we offer to them" (p. 15).

Autistic self-advocates provide the most compelling evidence of their motor planning challenges, which is often referred to as apraxia. In his book, *Anatomy of Autism*, Diego describes the nature of his apraxia at the age of nine:

My brain and body don't communicate messages the way most typical peo-ples do. As one of my classmates put it, it's like when you lose the Wi-Fi con-nection and your YouTube video stops loading. This is a really big pain in my butt. It is the reason why I can't talk or write. It is the reason why learning new skills is like running up an escalator the wrong way. This is also the rea-son why people think I'm not capable but I understand everything you want me to do [Peña, 2017, p. 11].

Researchers like Donnellan et al. suggest that Diego's motor difficulties are not so unique. Other families around the world have discovered that their children have been "locked in a silent prison," as Ido Kedar puts it, once they learn to type to communicate. Their sensory-movement challenges may explain why an autistic student requires physical, tactile, and visual prompting by a communication partner. These kinds of supports can mean the difference between pointing to random letters on a keyboard and executing purposeful motor movements to spell words with intent. In Kedar's (2011) keynote speech to the Los Angeles Autism Walk Now, he argued:

> I want people to know that not speaking is not the same as not thinking; that poor fine motor is not the same as not thinking; that impulsive actions are different than not understanding right from wrong; that poor facial affect is not the same as not having feelings; that boring people to death is denying them life, liberty, and the pursuit of happiness [para. 6].

Making a Decision About Diego's Communication

After being denied support for his communication at Diego's prior school, the decision to transition to a new school was difficult but necessary. In making this life-changing transition for Diego we stood firmly rooted in our decision to stick to our principles. While we feared a repeat performance of unsupportive and combative teachers, thankfully, the new principal and Diego's teachers did not disappoint us. They were willing to take a chance on educating Diego—the only nonspeaking child in his school who used a method of communication unfamiliar to them. They met with Diego, his communication partner, our new behavioral team, and my husband and me, treating us like equal members of Diego's team. They asked us questions about how they could support him in the classroom, honoring his need for a communication partner, a letter board, choice board, iPad—whatever he needed to access the curriculum and communicate. Diego's access to communication resulted in incredible opportunities to participate in rigorous curricula in general education and gifted education programs. Further, he could finally interact with others and cultivate meaningful relationships with his family, teachers, and peers. Diego began to thrive. In third grade, he wrote and published his first book, *Anatomy of Autism*. In it, Diego marveled at the change in his life after experiencing stellar support from his communication partner, Amanda, and his educational community.

He wrote, "I have experienced both judgement and freedom. When I was judged my wings were bound by the low expectations and I could not succeed. Now that I am free to be autistic, I soar" (Peña, 2017, p. 5).

My husband and I will do whatever it takes to give Diego access to communication, enabling him to stake his claim on using his voice. These efforts continue to require fierce advocacy. Without regret, we have fought tooth-and-nail with teachers, administrators, and therapists who attempted to dismiss and deny Diego's communication. We understand that professionals will continue to question these methods until they are rigorously studied and published in peer-reviewed journals. I am the first to believe in well-designed research studies. As an academic, I also believe in being open to new possibilities, ideas, and presuming competence in all individuals on the spectrum. After all, presuming competence, Donnellan (1984) argued long ago, is "the least dangerous assumption" (p. 141). That is, in the absence of reliable data about a student's intelligence, presuming competence is an assumption that, even if incorrect, has the least grievous effects on a child's life-long outcomes.

Without the presumption of competence, I would have never exposed Diego to RPM. He would not be where he is today with regard to sharing his inner thoughts about how autism affects his ability to sit still during long periods of classroom instruction (e.g., "Hope to very soon wave goodbye to stims [self-stimulatory behaviors]"; "Paying attention is tiring"), or articulating unusual and playful ideas at the age of 5 (e.g., "Eight elephants play in a new kind of ecosystem"). I would not know the level of depth of thought and curiosity hidden in his mind. Through his writings, Diego's voice is now being heard. His access to communication allows him to be a part of life decisions and choices made *with* him, not *for* him. The chapters that follow provide further evidence that autistic individuals who choose to use alternative modes of communication must be supported, empowered, and heard.

SECTION 1

Escaping the Institutionalization Mindset

Finding My Voice
Through Typing

TRACY THRESHER

Tracy Thresher is a native Vermonter who lives and works in Vermont. Tracy began using Facilitated Communication in 1990 and was one of the first individuals with autism in Vermont to be introduced to the method. He has presented at local, statewide and national workshops and conferences. Tracy is an employee of Washington County Mental Health Services and has consulted with local schools and adult service agencies, mentors high school students and adults with communication challenges, is a member of the Vermont Statewide Communication Task Force, and the WCMHS Communication Alliance. Tracy additionally performs free-lance work for Green Mountain Self-Advocates and works with the Well-spring Guild as a Master Trainer. Tracy and his friend Larry travel the world promoting their documentary Wretches & Jabberers *in an effort to change the World's view of disability to one of positivity. Tracy wants to thank Harvey Lavoy and Erin Rose for their strong and steady support in helping him put his story into words. Working on this project has been a meaningful journey and Tracy is hopeful that talking about experiences will amplify our message of inclusion and presumed intelligence. You can follow Tracy on his blog: www.wretchesandjabberers.org/tracy*

Don't underestimate me. I know more than I say, think more than I speak, and notice more than you realize.

I am Tracy Thresher, a man with autism who moves sideways through the world. What that means is that my mind and body are not always connected or working together. Thinking about what I want to do, and then actually doing it can be extremely difficult, if not impossible at times. My body takes over and shifts me into auto-mode, causing my thinking brain to shut down. My journey through life has been the bumpiest ride ever—not really fun like an amusement park ride, but more like a scary drop from the sky type of ride.

I have lived in Barre, Vermont, all of my life and was raised by my strong-willed parents, Susan and Hilton Thresher. Their lives have been centered on supporting my needs as I have autism. It has been a difficult disability to live with and I am still at a place, even though I am over fifty years old, where I cannot always accept myself. What my experience has been with trying to communicate before typing was frustration, erratic behavioral times to get my way, and helplessness. Now when typing I can self-express and connect with others in a way that was not possible before. With typing I am able to get my words out and let people know what I am thinking and feeling.

I share my story so that perhaps people will learn that I am intelligent and that other people with autism are intelligent too. We are inside our minds with much to say but our autism gets in the way and it is the only thing people see. It moves my anxiety up the ladder thinking about wasted years trying to show my ability to communicate. I get so angry thinking about it! I can show you my intelligence with typing; otherwise I would not be able to. Before 1990 it was very mind boggling for me and my family. They meant well but didn't know their real son. Those who tried to teach me thought I didn't understand them and some thought I was retarded.

Here is my journey.

Early Signs of Intelligence

I want to let you know first that I am not retarded; the world simply looks different from my experience. I do not speak, because I have autism. Autism means that I have a difficult time controlling my movements. It means that I find it difficult to do ordinary things that are quite easy for others. Most people take their ability to talk for granted and I take my inability to talk quite seriously. I live with it every day—it is always there each time someone wants to read my thoughts.

As a child, not being able to express myself was like being in a world of silence. I couldn't tell people what I liked and didn't like. People thought I was retarded, that I didn't understand what was being said to me. It was frustrating and made me angry and I withdrew. What could I do but wallow in my silent world with the world seeing only autism? The world saw the autism before typing and guess what? I acted autistic much of the time—without a meaningful way to express myself I could really only try and fail—what great frustration was that!

It is widely believed that people with autism can't learn to read and that many of us lack intelligence. I am here to tell you this is not true; we are more than capable of learning to read. Poor speech, problems with movement, and lack of natural learning opportunities interfere and prevent people with autism from learning to read and demonstrating the ability to communicate. Time and again, it is assumed that people with difficulty speaking are illiterate as well and that is simply not the case. I was, at a very young age, able to read letters, words, and numbers at lightning speed. I listened to the radio, watched television, and read magazines and newspapers. My loving Mom and grandmother, more than anyone in my childhood, taught me by reading to me. I also soaked up trivia from Jeopardy and language from Wheel of Fortune. Sesame Street was lots of happy friendly characters in my early lost boy days, leaping letters from PBS to my linguistic mind. Open up the learner's world, and it's amazing what can happen—the life force takes over and learning happens.

My experience with literacy was quite meaningful to me because I could learn about the world and how things worked. Pressing the world to see I could read was not an easy task. I hid my skills and only my mother had a sense of my reading. The best she could tell were signs like my studying the TV guide, turning the calendars the first day of each month, and getting the newspaper from the mailbox each day to read in my room. These were small signals that communicated to my mother that I was reading. It was not work I truly demonstrated until I started typing around age 23, and even then it took years before I could read out loud my typed words to show how intelligent I am.

Education Prison

Inclusion is necessary for children to grow in their social skills. Typing out my thoughts on inclusion brings out such old memories that time cannot erase. The isolation of seclusion hurts my spirit to this day. I think the biggest difference between being a student now and when I was a student in the 1970s and '80s would be that there are more resources available to parents today. Inclusion and appropriate accommodations in school were not a reality then. In my day, mom was told to put me in an institution, but thankfully she didn't listen. My mother chose to keep me at home so I could go to school. I was a student in the system from about age 5 until 22 and they were by no means years I want to repeat. The sad truth is my intelligence went undetected for far too long. It was a difficult time for me because there was no clear vision on how to teach me and little did they know I was a sponge taking everything in.

As a kid, I became so hard to deal with due to the fact that I was not being academically stimulated by interesting adventures of the mind. Jigsaw puzzles wasted precious time that I craved to be exploring mathematics, literature, and poetry. Little bits of history trickled through my keen-on-eavesdropping ears. For most of my days I was taken out of the class and isolated in my school environment. Often in a special classroom doing boring puzzles, I was an intelligent person doing rote time fillers and missing out on adventures of learning and particularly lacking in friendships with others. My teachers did not know how to handle my energy and I used my behavior a lot to get my needs met. My behavior was my ticket to communication. I felt like I did not have any control in my school life so I took matters into my own hands and I gave them a run for their money by eloping and leaving class when no one was paying attention.

I would always head in the direction of my home in hopes my mother would see what I was trying to communicate which was that schooling and teaching methods were not working for me. When I was older and making my way out of the education prison I was grouped together with others who had disabilities and this was isolation in the worst way. It made me angry and there were times when I would run away and the whole time I was thinking this cannot be my life.

I always felt like the education professionals did not really understand my behavior and it felt like my behavior determined who I was back then. I simply did not have another way to communicate. My keen ears could not filter out the pain of bullying. The teachers many times were equally at fault with the retardation label. Once the "R" word was pinned on me it basically felt like school was just a jail to suffer through. I desperately needed someone to come and rescue me from the prison of no communication and create an escape route to the land of free thoughts through supported typing.

How tragic to feel my mind shriveling like an unused muscle. When atrophy set in, survival mode took me to dark tunnels of despair. What power I lost by not having a proper education. I started typing to express hidden thoughts much later in life and I do think I would have experienced school differently if my communication could have been supported. I was in my twenties when my life took a path towards communication and I was chosen to be a part of a facilitated communication (FC) project. It was scary and exciting to have the foundation of a new thing in my life.

Taming the Beast

I want to treat people to my interior thinking. My speech is unreliable and the words are stuck in my head fighting to come out. I experience big time problems with anxiety, impulsive movement problems (poor impulse control), perseveration*, high muscle tone*, and lack of proprioception*. This affects everything I do in life. Sometimes I think saying the words is what will convince others of how I really do understand. But of course, I can't say the words and passively stand alone hoping the person that is trying to communicate with me will see that I want social contact, relationship, and conversation. With a respectful favorite communication partner I can experience those things. Without people satisfying my meaningful typing conversations I am at risk as being labeled as not understanding, not wanting to communicate, or wanting to do something else.

I was introduced to FC by Bill Ashe and later supported by Alan Kurtz. It was a wonderful time in my life because for the very first time,

I was being seen as someone with something to say. Bill and Alan presumed my competence and the feeling of being spoken to in an intelligent manner was exhilarating. My inner thoughts, for so long had hidden in my mind looking for light like trees needing to flourish. My true communication jumping out on thin strips of paper from my Canon Communicator was like first steps, shaky building of freeing my mind. They understood my intelligence, and it was not easy, but we pushed through my sometimes crazy behavior and I could pass reliable thoughts. Harvey Lavoy came to be my communication partner later on, and this was the beginning of a great friendship. To be connected to Harvey through the hard waking-from-the-old-Tracy was my emergence from insanity. Over many years, we honed our skills.

I admit I had a rocky start with FC. I have learned that movement issues mean something and that people interpret my actions as if I wanted to do them. My lack of impulse control, my going too hard at the letters, my problems with perseveration, and my pesky echolalic speech are things that get in the way of my ability to demonstrate my intelligence. In the beginning of learning to type, connecting to old memories pushed up my anxiety, making tough work for my facilitators.

Communication has been a big-time complicated journey that involves finding capable support staff to learn about my communication. The movement is first controlled by me, with communication partners that know how to support me correctly. The correct way is by holding my arm firmly, stopping me from easy irritating things, like my name and CBS sports. I can type those familiar things without touch because they are simply frozen in my motor system and just take over; it is not intentional thoughtful typing. Yes, there are many things I can type without being touched. But to type my true thoughts I need someone to hold my arm and be firm moving me beyond the typed echoes and perseverative patterns. With typing to express myself, I must really focus and pay close attention to what I am typing. Doing that while dealing with lack of body part connectivity, moving to the letters too hard, shifts in focus, and sensory issues popping up like sounds—you can see why it is nerve-racking hard.

I have high tone and I need much support to get organized in my typing movement. High muscle tone is the way my body is wired up and I go way too hard when typing. I also have proprioception challenges, which means I do not always know where my body is in space. Without support I go too fast and pound out automatics that are not my intelligent thoughts. The same is true for my speech. My spoken "yes" is mostly unreliable. However, my spoken "no" is reliable. Most of the time I just can't stop the word yes from popping out of my mouth; it is autism's hold on my speech.

One of the barriers to speaking out and being heard has been learning to work with new facilitators; they don't always know what to do and have to be told little bits of information at a time. It's hard to deal with someone who isn't familiar with me, or me with them, or with FC.

The problem of working with new facilitators is looking for the words and they look right back at you, but they are stuck and they don't come out. The hard thing about this is that people interpret my movement as intentional; the going-too-fast, hitting-too-hard, looking-away-when-spoken-to and even my limited, pesky speech patterns. That is extremely irritating! Going up the ladder of anxiety is a familiar course for me when I am on sensory overload and with lack of intentional movement I get stressed as well, making it hard to think and communicate what is going on in my mind. What will come out are typed perseverations and echoed phrases. Does anyone know what that feels like? That is anxiety at its highest!

It is extremely difficult dealing with the world with no speech. I can't express myself unless someone supports my typing and there are only a few people that can support reliable typed thoughts. This creates a great deal of anxiety for me and makes me angry at times, but the learning is damn worthwhile when I can let someone know what I am thinking.

I have been using FC for about 25 years now. It has been a long journey but I am working towards independence now. I communicate by typing on a computer with Intellikeys, a letter board, or iPad. I am typing with touch on my shoulder with two of my facilitators, and often they let go when I have a good rhythm. It is slow but steady progress. I would describe it as having a huge impact on how people see me. In the days when I was given more support I think my intelligence was questioned more and people were wondering if these were my thoughts. I am at a place where I will continue fading support and hope to get a handle on some of my impulsive movements.

Life Goals

I want people to know that not being able to talk doesn't mean there's a lack of understanding, or that the person doesn't want to share what they are thinking. Letting people know what my dreams, wishes, and desires are has helped me manage my anxiety. Not being able to speak doesn't take away the desire and need to have respect and the attention of others.

I want to tell you that my life experiences have been plentiful but really have included me making my own paths by seeking out ways on my own. The impact of learning to speak up and have a voice has been quite meaningful for me. I have typed life goals and dreams that have actually come true. One dream of mine was to go to church and be baptized. I told my mother this and it happened. I have been able to meet with my pastor and discuss God and the Bible because religion is very important to me.

My family has supported me by providing a home for much of my adult life. I made the decision to move out a number of years ago because I felt suffocated at home. I love my mom and dad dearly; however I wanted to be free and independent. When I was able to voice this I told my mom I was moving out. It was one of the most difficult and trying times in my life, but I know I made the right decision because otherwise I would not be where I am today. I am learning to do the things I want to—teaching others about autism and FC and movement differences. These are things I've wanted to do and now it's happening!

The biggest world experience for me was making the movie *Wretches & Jabberers* and traveling to Sri Lanka, Japan, and Finland. That tested my ability to self-regulate and connect with people in three different countries. I found out I could negotiate airports, customs, long flights, and enjoy sushi. Doing *Wretches & Jabberers* propelled my purpose to one of thinking more globally. I had often wondered how it was for people living with Autism in other countries. It is my feeling that I needed this journey to discover my true purpose in life.

The first trip was to visit my long-time friend Chammi in Sri Lanka; we met many moons ago in Syracuse and forged a strong bond as typing gurus. We presented together at many conferences and workshops paving the way for presuming competence. It was wonderful to spend time with Chammi in his homeland. What I learned was that he was an outcast in Sri Lanka and educated by his mother. That was a likely hard thing for him to deal with after living in the United States for several years. What I learned is that other countries are far behind us when it comes to inclusion and educating individuals with autism and lack speech.

For example, Naoki Higashida from Japan had to be home schooled because the regulations would not allow him to be educated in school. In this technological world Naoki reached out to me from Japan. Through email I was able to connect with Naoki and impart knowledge, like teaching him the title of self-advocacy. The technology that is available is our way of connecting to others. In Japan I had the great opportunity to share my vision of changing the world's view of how they perceived people with disabilities. Together Naoki and I shared our stories of having intelligence inside of us that is not often placed highly in the perception of society.

We also visited Finland where I met Henna and Antti and we forged a strong typing relationship. They were very lovely people that were hungry for time to type and connect, which didn't happen often. To be trapped in a life lacking in adventure; locked into routines makes for poor quality of life. Henna is the perfect candidate for educating and mentoring others. To limit Henna's opportunity starves the community.

On my journey with traveling the world to film *Wretches & Jabberers* I was able to release the old dark cloak of autism. What an experience that was, and since the movie has been released I have traveled the world with Harvey Lavoy, Larry Bissonnette, and Pascal Cheng—as the Fab Four—typing pearls of wisdom to educators, parents, professionals, and students to change their views of disability. My life is now mine to teach others about overcoming communication barriers. I believe it is important to break down barriers of labeling to move to inclusion.

I am so amazed that I broke free of the trapped-in-my-head angry man I had become. Meeting Monk Hogen while filming *Wretches &*

Jabberers in Japan gave me such clarity, shining brilliance on my purpose to make education accessible to all. During our visit to his temple, Monk Hogen said to me:

> What we teach in Buddhism is that the person who can set a purpose in your life is you, you are the only person who can set the purpose in your life. You are born in the United States, or you are born as a male, but it's beyond your control and you don't think about that, you just accept the fact. And after you accept the fact, you search for the meaning or purpose of your life, and that will be the purpose of your life.

The moving words he said to me inspired much in my spirit and I responded that:

> I completely understand and that makes so much sense. I have decided that my purpose in life is to show that people like me are intelligent, and that is how I came to this place and time. Meeting with you has now brought me life force.

Now my typing to audiences of diverse folks from professionals, to educators, to families trying to navigate through to more open communication is healing salve for me. Typing is my true voice and I have taken my power to kids to educate them and their supports.

Self-Advocacy for Inclusion and Communication

My life has changed dramatically since the release of our film. I now have the beginning of the life I dreamt of. I have inspired others through my blog to communicate their stories. Mostly I was given the message I needed. For me the message is that I have to teach my fellow wretches-in-arms that we need to join forces to get our message on the minds of others. When I think about my purpose in life, I know it is having the perseverance to be a leader to those in need of guidance and purpose. I had a meltdown thinking of the lost opportunities in my life, but I now try to think of the present to move on to the better times of inclusion for all people.

My mind has been extremely focused on the power of inclusion. Inclusion, like communication, is paramount to healthy children and long term success. I want educators to understand that all children benefit from inclusion because all children can make contributions with proper supports. Inclusion is not mainstreaming. More than idealistic political correctness, it is celebrating our interconnectedness. Lessons of humanity lift our social fabric to magical tapestries where natural abilities may soar. Like Larry and I have communicated to diverse audiences in our travels, we are first men with intelligence. Like Larry says: "More like you than not." Judge us not by our diagnosis. One of the best questions Larry and I have been asked was, "What do you tell parents of kids with disabilities who oppose inclusion?" My response: "What kind of life are we talking about with seclusion and sameness and focused on disability? Now that we are here, it's due to being included. What hope is there without seeing us in the mix?"

I have known for a long time that I wanted to educate other people living with communication challenges to advocate for themselves. By teaching others to self-advocate and make their voices heard, I feel like my life has purpose. It is wonderfully boosting to my confidence to have the ability to teach others; we all have intelligence that we have to give to the world. For educators, I recommend teaching students the power of self-advocacy and speaking up to meet their goals in life.

Even though my friends and I possess intelligent ideas, the people in the educational system for the most part have historically not understood how to educate us. Teaching kids, parents, and teachers is one of my goals. I want to plot out the path toward training teachers to look at their students with a wide lens of possibility. The lens is the way to see the pupil's intelligence that is always there but sometimes has difficulty coming out through communication. It is imperative that educators think about presuming competence and look for ways to see the intelligence in all of us. The student should not have to prove they are capable of learning. The school needs to provide the educational experiences to teach the student literacy, communication, and skills to be a learner.

It really is a wide open world with a reliable way to communicate. I want to be a life force in changing people's attitude towards disability. I am a self-advocate who is inspired by those who want to share their voice. In my profession as an advocate I travel around the country and beyond to teach people about advocacy, autism, movement differences, and communication. I live, breathe, and think about quality of life initiatives. I am passionate about where our country is going as far as education and services for all citizens is concerned. My work is cut out for me with travel, typing, and presenting to teach the presumption of competence, and I am fired up with possibility.

I am so honored to now be recognized for my work. To know others value the work I have done to break down the barriers that have been preventing people from living the lives they deserve is wonderful. I stand before audiences in amazement that I have progressed from the young boy who teachers overlooked—with the hard eyes of being bothered—to being looked upon as a wise leader of teaching others. The presumption of competence is the key to opening the barriers people may have in their minds. Working in this field of communication and rights for all jazzes my motivation to connect and work with as many people as humanly possible. As our society is exposed to the thinking, and true reality, that presuming competence only increases one's quality of life, I can rest easy at night knowing that I have done my part.

Popular in the Movies

Larry Bissonnette Becomes
Writer of His Life Story

LARRY BISSONNETTE

Larry Bissonnette is a disability rights advocate and artist who lives in Milton, Vermont. He has been painting and drawing since he was a young child and exhibits his art regularly both locally and nationally. Larry is both the subject and writer of an award winning film about his life, called, My Classic Life as an Artist: A Portrait of Larry Bissonnette *(http://sproutflix.org/all-films/my-classic-life-as-an-artist/; 2005). Most recently, he starred in a feature length documentary directed by Gerardine Wurzburg about adults with autism called* Wretches and Jabberers *(www. wretchesandjabberers.org/; 2010). Over the past 20 years, he has been a featured presenter at many national educational conferences and has written and spoken on the topics of autism, communication and art. Larry states, "I want to thank patient, with my longwinded typing style, Pascal for pushing me to be a writer of my life experiences and lessons learned from bringing up my intelligent thoughts into the world of real communication."*

My Life in the Institution

I am a survivor of low expectations, with my intelligence and artistic ability now planting my image in practically *People Magazine* status. What is possibly trailing my work as an artist, movie star and part-time speaker at conferences is the path I took to this place. Use of assistance of people in my past to write my story will be hard because people probably saw me as a mentally retarded person and would not have treated me as intelligent or potentially painter of pictures to be hung in a museum. Approaching of writing my story will lead from perceptions of my experiences, poorly remembered for exact details but precisely recalled for feelings. I will lead you through looking at my years in the institution, leaving to have amounts of community life, and now looking at my career as an artist and movie star.

My Early Life

I was born to parents who worked hard to live the easiest life possible. Our home wasn't fancy but we lived comfortably in Winooski, Vermont, better known as a poor community compared with the more prosperous city of Burlington. It was probably a different experience for my parents to try parenting an autistic boy at a time without services and programs. I was limited in my social and academic skills and did not have the opportunity to learn the skills needed to play with other kids and learn in picture and letter-rich classrooms. There were no teachers or schools in my community that used the philosophy of inclusion and acceptance of my disability. Looking at most of the children with autism at this time you could write the same story.

So it was worked out with my parents that the ideal place for me was an institution. I was sent to the Brandon Training School, very likely without another option to look at in the future. This happened when I was probably around eight years old and it lasted for ten or more years before I was placed in another institution, the Waterbury State Hospital. This was an institution more going for intensive medication so that bad behaviors would not prevail over actions of a person. People looked partly at my autism as looking weird and acting inappropriately. Appearances of my artistic ability weren't that frequent and it was the perception of most people that nothing was learned by me because my intelligence was limited.

The Brandon Training School looked like a farm-like environment but positioned there were buildings of an institution instead of fields full of crops. People walked to move from building to building but the world of people who were not disabled was closed off. Time was planned out in terms of meals and learning to socialize was not included in the daily schedule. Everyone planted themselves in the day room and did not interact with each other. Meals were the most interesting part of the patterned days. We had poorly cooked meat lacking in taste, vegetables, and some rice or potatoes in the dining room. Time in the bedroom area was lacking in the type of privacy that I now have. In this place, we looked at each other like prisoners. The people who lived with me were not potentially dangerous. They were just loud and lacked respect towards the personal space.

Sometime I might have worked once in the sheltered workshop there and would have learned purposeful patterns of doing work but I could not stay free of bad behavior and had to leave, potentially ordering me into category of low possibility for remaking of my status in the institution.

It was nothing people who worked in Brandon did to me to make me poorly able to live in the community. It was really the patterns of the lack of openings to learning and socializing with others that pushed my growth as a person back into the apple core of autism. So I missed the boat of social inclusion that might have helped new growth of people skills in me. I am thinking now that I might have learned to connect with people better if autistic production of language was shaped by words lots of people would say in day to day conversation.

Personal Perspectives on Autism

Understanding my life in the institution looks possible if one looks at the ways in which society has treated people with autism, especially those like me with poor behavior and communication skills. The history on approaches to teaching people with lots of repetitive speech presents a picture of people lacking the intelligence to learn to read complex text and write sophisticated in language, prose, and poetry.

It was many hours of TV watching that placed knowledge about the words and ideas people in lettered, mainstream society used in my geared for print brain. Larry liked watching the big station newscasts and prosperous for smart people game shows like Hollywood Squares. Seeing words on the screen, paired with professionally spoken lines of anchors of news and perpetually joyful, ageless in looks, hosts, plentifully articulate, netted for me a picture of a world outside the institution that was potentially available to me in the event I ever left the institution. However, practicing the use of my literacy was limited to writing rote lists of words, which were not Pippy Longstocking like in creative expression, but meaningless production of autistic patterns.

Issuing me, torturing my identity as a person, label of psychiatrically disturbed individual made me think of myself as person whose feelings of anger about life grew out of often held belief that my disability was purely the positioning of maladaptive genes in my body rather than the isolation from society and people that life in the institution placed me in. Without an idea of what experts in psychology and education said about me in my records, it was impossible to predict with any certainty how I was going to be treated in the future. Opportunities I might have had to learn communication skills got shoved into the corner of special education never to be accessed by me.

Working on my patterns of learning of social skills today in a regular school environment is what might have helped me then. I wanted to know about my disability in terms of how I could overturn the tables of poor behavior and learn pleasing to others manners and ways of interacting with real intelligent words. Working on learning these things later on in life has happened and now I know it's my autism rather than an illness of psychological roots that causes my lack of acting like a person with intelligence. So issuing me the labels of movie star and artist is a little like the remaking of an old movie and totally leading the public to a new understanding of its themes with an improved script and greatly perfected by advances in technology, sound, and visual effects.

Life in the Community

It was my good fortune to be selected for leaving the institution at a time when the popularity of life in the community was rising. People's attitudes about institutions changed perhaps because, potentially, autism was better understood. I wanted placement of labels to open with positive language and not the negatively slanted words used to state problems of behavior as psychological disturbance. Autism was beginning to show up in the writing of professionals and mass media and this portrayal helped the public to realize that life in an institution lacked meaningful activities for the people who lived there. It was out in the community with the right support and worthwhile opportunities for learning that would enable the social integration of people like me and our achievement of work careers and creative endeavors to happen.

There were also financial advantages to moving people into the community and not paying for a large institution, landscaped with many structures and staffed with many workers whose reason to exist was to maintain those structures and not the people living in them. It wasn't as expensive as paying for all the workers and bureaucrats at the institution. So even though there was an openness to people living in the community, realistically the money and resources needed had to become a category of neutral budget.

So I was able to leave the institution and live in an apartment with another person. Starting this new life was quite partnered with becoming independent in many tasks around the house like doing laundry, cooking meals and making my bed. Doing these tasks brought me a sense of accomplishing things that people in the community took for granted. Allowing lots of variety with rote tasks also helped my figuring out how to be more flexible with participation in tasks at home.

The potential for working on social skills that were needed to be able to make it in regular community situations was there too. I had opportunities to practice these skills. I learned to act more appropriately going into a store or restaurant. Working on more playful sounds of pleasure picking my movements out to not call attention to nuttier side of my autism was potentially an important skill that I mastered. It was possibly the time in my life with the most progress towards living more independently.

The placement with my family occurred later on after I had moved into the community in the late nineteen eighties. It was the closing down of the apartment program that led to my family strongly making the case that I had to keep company with regular people out in the community, and plans needed to be made linking me to community services. My mom and the head of family, my sister, Sally, lived together out in the country for probably close to fifteen years. With my aptitude for art, I had people who were interested, of course, in working with an accomplished artist but my serious lack of social and communication skills prevented me from being a participant in all community situations.

Discovering Communication

Without an effective way to communicate thoughts and ideas, planting myself in the land of, ordered by social interaction, community was going to be hard. So, in 1991, one of my professionally trained teacher of communication skills staff, Pascal Cheng, provided me with the opportunity to experience a new revolutionary communication technique called facilitated communication. Pascal needed opportunities for practicing new professional learning and met my communication challenges by putting me inside the world of meaningful language and intelligent thought through typing.

Working on my ability to express myself trained my mind to make patterns of thoughts and ideas into words on a computer screen. Partnering the movement that was necessary to arrange letters in the right sequence for purposeful typing on a keyboard with high expectations for totally within my abilities language production was Pascal's role. He marked out time to practice typing on a primitive keyboard looking to make needed changes in my movements towards the letters, lessening automatic, issued without thought, responses and increasing my ability to produce intelligent and purposeful ones.

It was not easy at first because language that I was letting out with my big loud voice was often lacking real spontaneity. Older, patterned by repetition words and phrases, pre-dominated my communication. Planning lots of words to produce an opinion with my big voice was not easy to learn to do but letting people know that I needed to eat relied more on an intuitive set of words which did not require me to plan out my words. So my speech worked really well if supper was two minutes late. My feelings of hunger were let out like birds leaving a cage the moment the door opens. However, more often, my echolalic words would just come down my pipes like a pre-programmed train that was way off its itinerary.

Pascal lowered the boom on my impulsive responding by using light physical support to slow my movements down. This spotted my words on a platform of controlled language processing. This was more than just a pleasing experience for me. It was quite the profound revelation for me and nothing was more perfectly transitioned to real change than this. Learning to type more typical language using less support, and linking many sentences in a row without stopping are my goals now.

Introduction to Art

Doing art was a way for me to annex interesting images of everyday things present in the family-less institution and make use of my hands. Art-making motions were done in the day rooms of the institution with crayons and calling for sharpener colored pencils. Appearance of markers and paints occurred later on with painting paper and very large boards when I was an adult. Occupying time in the institution was the initial purpose as it was somewhat boring and people working there operated at a place picturing people as numbers on a competence scale. Because of my behavior and perseverative speech I was seen as a lower functioning resident with my autism not yet understood. New look at my artmaking as demonstration of real artistic ability did not happen until I had left the institution and began attending art workshops taught by professional artists who pushed me to move from being a potentially talented person to becoming a passionate lover of good art.

I made good-to-exhibit, absolutely primitive, better fit for outsider art shows, drawings and made wood-like construction pieces frames that skated around the images like picket fences lining a house to set off its pretty structure. Opening this part of my artistic self to the public view led to my career as an artist of worth and placed me on a path towards people accepting me prominently in society. It was Larry the artist now rather than Larry the wild and crazy autistic guy.

Planting new painting work of museum level quality in local and national exhibitions of artists of all labels is my long-term plan. My more beauty driven goal is to make pleasing to the eye drawings on a daily basis because the power of art making comes from picking out visionary ideas about the world around you and mowing them into ragged movements of your hands to produce a work of aesthetically pleasing, naturally wrought and driven by impulse and intuition, expression. With art, people can look at my abilities without focusing on my autism moving Larry's status from the autistic guy who can paint towards that of the artist of intelligence and great creativity.

Becoming a Movie Star

In 2009, the opportunity to star in a movie with Tracy—learning to be like George Clooney—Thresher was presented to me by noted disability and socially conscious film maker Gerry Wurzburg who wanted to create a story about really oddball but highly intelligent adults with autism whose lack of meaningful speech led them to find their articulation of thoughts and ideas through typing. The work we did to make the film took us to three different countries, Sri Lanka, Japan and Finland, basing us in a pattern with constant communication and out of our normal routine experiences. It was a once in a lifetime opportunity for me, even if I never visited McDonald's in our lots of new foods sampled on the journey.

People in the world of autism picture themselves as tourists in the land of normality, so going to a foreign country picks this scenario up and shoots it into the land of para-normality. Probably most experiences of autistic tourists don't involve airplanes, so picture us in space capsules and that would bring our experiences of intercontinental travel to your level. Little did I understand about the countries we were going to and working without worrying too much with Pascal to arrange the travel schedule was like needing to shut my eyes and leap into an unknown pool of deep water trusting that I would be thrust to the surface still alive with more elation than fear.

Going to these new lands placed me under new living conditions, moving me to make huge adjustments in eating and living habits. Pleasing to the eye luxury hotels did alleviate my anxieties about changes in my routine especially when productively kept busy with moviemaking activities. Ordering different foods in lots of restaurants worked on shifting my attitudes about needing set routines. We were fed on many, excellently made meals of local foods. Many people would kill for a specially prepared meal like sushi. However, making my day in culinary heaven this was not, but the experience of positioning raw octopus on my fork for slow consumption provided with a personally meaningful cultural experience not found in American fast food restaurants. Tracy was looking for an adventure, natural for a sushi man.

Our days were less than ordered with normal daily routines and we pin-balled around with film crews working like a team of long days into the night letter carriers. I operated on lots of proud waves of excitement initially and throughout the project as I could see how Tracy and I used our typed words to drive the story. I was pretty awed that we actually appeared like coherent communicators. We were driven into typing frenzies by director, Gerry Wurzburg. We did big inspirational presentations on looking at intelligence as a communication partnership with inner thoughts and ideas. I learned to read my typing and found that I am better at saying Budweiser than tough going words like psychological.

Weathering the changes in my routine towards participating fully in the film making was not easy but it was potentially the most rewarding thing that I have ever have done, not because we were the stars but because people who saw the film had to now look at autism with different perspectives starting with understanding that intelligence moves in different ways and meets communication at the door of, more precise than speech, iPad typed on, words. People could also see themselves in our experiences and look at disability as one side of the same human collection of multi-colored stamps. Owning up to my lack of real experiences with partnering with professional film makers, I can truly say that working on this documentary led towards more people with autism making their appearances in movies and I am more proud of that as one of my legacies.

Looking Towards the Future

Other people with autism who communicate like I do might want to hear a few words of wisdom from me. Plentiful words of wisdom about behavior I cannot give but I can tell you how to lead a meaningful life in the community. People are always approaching me, peppering me with probing questioning about my life in the community and also my life as an artist as if the world I live in is an ideal situation with allowances for my autism and participation in the community. Attending events like concerts I do get to do and having a daily cup of coffee at a hip, non–Starbucks place I also get to do. I am grateful for these things and plan on them every day. Male people with autism suffer from the lack of George Clooney looks and personalities of the promoting ego type so it is hard to learn how to socially interact with women.

So you will have to learn life in the community early on. Play on the same playgrounds as other kids and look ahead to college and a career. Participating in everyday activities with peers teaches you social interaction. You must have friends to pull you along like people playing sports and having cheering to lead them towards victory. Malls might look all the same but learning how to socially interact meaningfully happens there for lots of young people so you should think about places that people frequent like your favorite coffee shop or hamburger joint. Going time again and again to McDonalds is not healthy but it does give you practice ordering or complaining about your badly cooked burger. You can let patterns of ordering lengthen into making wisecracks and listening to what lasting words you have for them about good friendship. So it's planting your roots like apple orchards in Vermont in your communities and practicing patterns of social interactions regularly with your iPad that will propel your voices into the bright future.

To others who communicate like I do, I say that learning to determine your road to self-actualization needs to start by creating words either through speech or sometimes fickle technology dependent, potentially printed out, typing and powerfully expressing out to others what you think and feel. You will have to make laps around the noisy field of jabberers with your typed words. Tapping on your iPad will lead to you being seen as the people who next to President Lincoln liberated the speechless and changed society for the better. So look towards positioning yourself in the world of letters and you will make it in society.

Defiantly Reclaiming
My Right to Learn

Amy Sequenzia

Amy Sequenzia is a non-speaking Autistic who writes about disability rights, civil rights, and human rights. Amy has presented in several conferences in the U.S. and abroad, and her work is featured in books about being Autistic and Disabled. Her first published work was as a contributor for the anthology Loud Hands, Autistic People Speaking. *In 2015, Amy co-edited an anthology of essays written by people who type, write, or point to letters to communicate,* Typed Words, Loud Voices, *and her work appeared on a book that is a resource for parents of Autistic children,* Real Experts. *She was a contributor on the book,* Speaking for Ourselves—Conversations on Life, Music, and Autism, *by Michael Bakan. Amy serves on the Board of Directors of the Autistic Self Advocacy Network (ASAN). She blogs regularly for Ollibean.com and the Autism Women's Network. All her online published work can be found on her blog nonspeakingautisticspeaking.blogspot.com. Amy thanks Adriana, her assistant, facilitator and cheerleader while Amy typed the words that appear in this chapter.*

Trigger Warning: mentioning of the R-word and other ableist slurs.

Diagnosis and Exclusion

I am autistic. I was born Autistic.
I have cerebral palsy.

I am epileptic. Epilepsy crept in my life first slowly, then with rage.

My development was delayed and my first diagnosis was cerebral palsy. It took me longer than most children to crawl and walk, I could never speak more than a few words, which did not become speech. I think it might have been echolalia.

When I was supposed to be learning how to play with other kids, I was having therapies to improve my muscle tone and motor skills. My family wasn't prepared to have a disabled child, and they did everything the doctors suggested, maybe hoping that the disability would be "hidden" if I were able to do things in a more "normal" way.

I went to school, a special education class. It wasn't good. I was abused at times, ignored at times. There wasn't any learning. I was clearly disabled but what was expected of me was that I should learn to be non-disabled.

That's right: I wasn't taught anything but the expectation was that I reacted to any event, changes or demands in a non-disabled way.

The next school wasn't much better, and I don't think I learned anything there either. I was already having seizures but they were under control. Adjustments in medication worked and I would be seizure free for a while. But medications have side effects, and the side effects of anticonvulsants can make everything more difficult—it can make someone lethargic, or it can cause confusion, or it can make someone agitated and anxious, for example.

It was around that time that I taught myself how to read. I learned the letters, and how to form words, while watching Sesame Street.

I wasn't planning on learning how to read. I don't think that "reading" is what I actually learned. I think it is more accurate to say that I learned how to love words, how to make all those letters come together to form colorful concepts in my head. I wasn't concerned about texts and messages. I think these came later.

As a very young girl, I was simply mesmerized by the colors and shapes those sounds—the sounds of each letter, and each word, the combination of letters to form words—brought to my brain.

I am not a visual learner. I learn better by listening to things. I am also a synesthete (something I didn't realize until a few years ago), so the sound of the letters and words created a unique beauty in my head. Even today, I don't read much. It is overwhelming to me, to focus on chunks of text, especially if the letters are small.

So, I learned words, something I would love forever, from Sesame Street. I think about this today and I realize that I probably was able to learn because the TV wasn't calling me names, pushing me, hitting me.

The characters in the show didn't assume I couldn't learn. I was accepted, I learned in my own time, and in my own way.

But nobody knew that. Nobody knew how to teach me in a way I could learn. Nobody thought I wanted to learn.

To most people, I was disabled and I was to be fixed. The only things that mattered to them was that I learned some "skills," that I learned how to ask to use the bathroom, that I learned how to look a little bit "normal."

Day after day I had to go to a school where I was seen as a burden, as "retarded," as a "difficult" child. Sometimes, the teachers treated me with kindness. I like to think that some of the people in school even liked me, the way a lot of people like small children. But I was also someone who gave them a hard time.

From my home movies, I can say that I was quite adorable. I always loved music and I liked all the singing—even if I wasn't able to sing. I also loved playful games, like peekaboo (I saw myself playing it in a home movie and I seemed very happy). Although I had happy moments, I remember being afraid of people a lot of the time.

To make things a little more complicated, I was about to receive another diagnosis. My parents were told I had some "behaviors." I don't remember what they called "behaviors" but I think I was crying a lot. I know that I was frustrated with everybody's inability to see me, and to understand me. I was tired of being hit and pushed, I was tired of being called names. I didn't understand the meaning of the slurs, but I could feel the intention when I was called "stupid."

After more doctors, more specialists and more tests, I received a diagnosis of PDD-NOS (Pervasive Developmental Disorder—Not Otherwise Specified) and later, after even more tests and a trip across country, I was diagnosed as Autistic.

Meanwhile the non-learning continued in the school that didn't believe in me.

I don't remember having an IQ test but since I already had a diagnosis of "Mental Retardation," the autism diagnosis only made people see me as unworthy of their time to teach me things that I was eager to learn.

But I was learning. I was listening and absorbing information that I would use later. At the time, I didn't know how to express my knowledge, how to make people understand me, how to use the neurotypical preferred way of communication. So I kept playing with letters and words in my head. I kept observing people, and making connections, and making sense of what happened all around me, while teachers and therapists ignored me. To them, I was like a puppy that needed to be trained to behave. That was the only way I would be accepted in their world.

Institutionalization and Disabled Schooling

In a way, the autism diagnosis changed the course of my life. There weren't any Autistic adults—at the time—speaking out about what it means to be Autistic, and autism was considered a "mystery." The doctors said I was never going to learn and that I should be placed in a facility. I was six years old when I was institutionalized. According to everyone, I was such a burden on my parents that they should simply let me be taken care of in a place for "people like me," and go have a life of their own. The message was that they deserved something better than a child who could never learn or become a real human being.

The place my parents chose—the "best" at the time—was a so-called Center for Autism. I call it a luxury institution. It was clean and beautiful. There were toys (for therapy, not for playing), a playground, clean walls, and smiling faces.

It also had locked doors, no learning, and unfriendly faces—when visitors were not around. Visitors, even family members, could not just show up, they had to schedule appointments and when they visited, they had to be escorted by a staff member at all times.

There wasn't any teaching there. Remember, I was deemed "unteachable," and unable to learn. There was compliance training, meaning that I was treated like a puppy, rewarded for desirable behavior, and punished for noncompliance. I think I was supposed to learn how to obey, without knowing why I had to obey.

Just like the schools I attended before this institution, I loved playtime with other children, and I loved the singing.

I wish they had seen how much I loved the music and the instruments.

As it was in the schools before this institution, I was verbally abused, and physically punished. I wish they had seen me, a human being.

I did learn one thing while there. I learned that I was not worthy.

Today, I know this is not true but institutionalized care is not supposed to teach us to value ourselves. It is not about our lives at all.

Institutionalized "care" is about non-disabled people celebrating their perceived superiority over us, the "not-quite-humans," while making us feel exactly like that: sub-humans.

A note about my parents: Even as they followed the guidance (or misguidance) of the doctors who rejected my humanity, they never stopped looking for better services and supports for me. Part of their relentlessness, was because of their own ableism—I was their only child, a very disabled child, and the "specialists" were certain that I had no future. I am sure they would have preferred a non-disabled child, or at least a child they could understand better. I don't hold a grudge and I am grateful for the times they did get it right.

I don't have bad feelings about them. I love them and they love me. My mom kept learning until she passed away, my dad keeps learning.

In their quest to make me "better," they researched and made it possible for me to be introduced to the method of communication that would allow me to show that I could learn, that I was learning.

I was lucky then and later I could teach them about being accepting of me.

That method was Facilitated Communication (FC).

People like to attach the word "controversial" to FC. As in: "the controversial method," or "FC is controversial."

To me, FC was never a controversy. From my first session, I was taught something. More than that, I could show that I was learning things through observation. I could let everyone know that I could spell words and have thoughts children my age had; I could let people know about my dreams and fears. FC makes my thoughts accessible to people who are used to typical forms of communication. It is my language.

The person who introduced me to FC taught me how to make the words I saw in my head known to other people. She had one assumption: that I could, and did, learn.

After that day, everything changed—and nothing changed. I had shown that I could learn, that I wanted to learn. But I was living in an institution, and institutions are not places where disabled people have intellectual stimulation, or where curiosity is rewarded. Institutions are about control, about making us act in ways non-disabled people consider acceptable.

The things we are taught in an institution are not meant to enrich ourselves, to make us question assumptions, or become critical thinkers. We are taught to dislike ourselves and believe that we are "less than."

So, for a few months, I remained in the non-learning environment, so excited and at the same time so frustrated that very few people were willing to look at me as a whole: an uncooperative body and a mind full of thoughts and questions.

They decided to focus on how to fix my bodily responses, while ignoring my brain, its connections as well as the lapses in connections, and how it related to my body.

Ignoring my eagerness to learn, and my ability to learn if given the supports was how they could keep seeing me as damaged, too disabled to have any value.

I left that place and hoped for more but the assumptions of incompetence were attached to me by "Very Important Specialists," by doctors who saw me as a disease, by teachers who never looked beyond the normalizing chart every student is supposed to be measured by. Those truths prevailed.

My body could not follow my brain. I was still undesirable and many people could not believe that someone so disabled, so "retarded," could show signs of thinking. It was easy to dismiss me as unable to learn because of how I looked, because of how my body reacted, or didn't react, to everything.

I was again placed in a special education class. Once more, teaching wasn't provided. Nobody cared if I was learning, and because nobody was interested in learning how to support my newly found communication method, I was silenced.

I went from not being able to let people know I could learn, and being institutionalized, to showing them that I could learn, then leaving the institution to go to a day school—and being silenced. There was never a single moment of real academic learning.

Then, something happened: someone did believe in me. It started as a traumatic event. A teacher told someone that I was "too retarded to understand anything." I heard it. I told (typed to) my mom, who talked to the teacher. That showed the teacher that I could, indeed, understand things. The teacher promised to work with me.

Hope. That was the feeling—Soon crashed by a furious attack on my brain.

The seizures would not stop. Hospitals, medications and doctors consumed me. There wasn't any energy left to learn. I know I was in intensive care units (ICUs) for many days. Every new medication brought all the side effects, and didn't stop the seizures. I don't remember much of anything related to schools for those two years of trying to stop the terror in my brain. I know I missed a lot of classes, and I probably didn't type much. I remember the fatigue, the fear, and the sadness.

Finally, I was prescribed a combination of medication that controlled the seizures. But the side effects left me lethargic, tired all the time, not really interested in learning.

If you have seizures, or if you take too many pills in order to not die of status epilepticus, you know that you need to train your brain, and fight with your body, to sync them with your wish to live a life of learning, discoveries, curiosity and connections.

My brain was tired.

My body was even more uncooperative.

I looked, and was, more disabled than before.

The first typing session that brought so much hope was two years before and I had to remember how to make my fingers point to letters again.

I went back to school where there was no learning, where I spent my days falling asleep because I became invisible to the teachers. They knew I could type and learn, but I needed more time, I needed more breaks, and I needed them to have more patience.

So, even if I had changed, and even if I had found a way to make people understand me, the way I was perceived hadn't changed.

I was considered difficult.

I was entering puberty and not a cute little girl anymore.

Some people looked at me with disgust. They didn't try to work with me.

The reality is that I was anxious and frustrated. When I was overwhelmed and reacted to the feeling of overwhelm, people only saw a "challenging behavior."

The school, the teachers and all involved with my education failed to understand that. So I spent my days not learning.

My parents were overwhelmed too. They didn't understand how my Autistic brain worked, and how tired my brain became after seizures.

They didn't understand why my body reacted in the way it did.

They didn't understand the concept of mind-body disconnect of their Autistic daughter.

But they also understood that my student life should be more than from bus to non-learning to lunch to non-learning to bus.

They kept looking for a place where I could learn and maybe prove to the Very Important Specialists that I wasn't unworthy. The answer came as a school that promised a respectful approach, an understanding of disabled children as full and complex human beings.

The school was in another state so I had to, again, move away from my parents.

The word for how I felt in that "school" is bored. The way they treated me was not different from how the so-called educators in the other schools and the institution treated me.

I was bored and alone. I was a pre-teen, so there wasn't a lot of playing and music anymore. Sometimes an instructor would take me to a music therapy session, but it was like a chore they had to fulfill, not something they were interested in learning about me.

All the "teaching" was about "life skills" and "personal care." I had to practice getting dressed, which can be hard when hands don't have the strength to pull things, or to hold things, or when it feels like your hands move in the opposite way the brain wants them to move.

I also had to go grocery shopping as part of my "learning." I just don't remember any real instruction given in those outings.

Everything I did was based on compliance training. I don't think they called it applied behavior analysis (ABA), and as I mentioned before, I don't remember events very well, only how I felt at the time, but I have seen some home videos and I can tell it was compliance based "training."

Two things might have contributed for the non-learning environment, besides the "school" being really bad: First, all the teachers and therapists inability to recognize that I am not a visual learner. They insisted on PECS (Picture Exchange Communication System). It was boring and exhausting. Boring because I wasn't interested in it. I should be typing, not looking at pictures. Exhausting because processing pictures is very hard, even when I choose what I want to see. In the PECS sessions, I couldn't choose anything. Defiantly, I refused to cooperate.

Second, the method of typing I use is facilitated communication (FC) and at that time there were so called "controversies" about the method. I am not going to talk about what those "controversies" were but they were damaging to people like me. The word of a few "experts" caused hysteria and unjustified condemnation of a method. No method of communication is wrong, even if there are some people who misuse such methods. These "experts" set about discrediting FC in the media. After that, a lot of people decided that they would not work with FC anymore. Maybe the school decided that this was more convenient for them, so I was, again, silenced.

With a program that insisted on a method that was difficult for me to understand, while mostly ignoring the method I had chosen, I spent the next four years not learning. I was 15 years old and had never been taught anything in any of the schools, and so-called schools, I had been to.

My parents were not satisfied. They kept fighting and looking for some meaningful education for me. The next school was a boarding "Special School," even farther away from home. I think that, despite a lot of ableism I was about to experience there, it was the first place where I was seen as a student, and not just a "tragic, very disabled and hopeless person."

It didn't start very well. I think that most of the decision makers in the school didn't really want me there. From the very beginning, many of the teachers and people around the campus were unwelcoming. After I left the place, I heard about how some people there talked about me. Some used words like "disgusting," and one doctor wrote on my file that I didn't have "human dignity."

Like in the other places I had been to, some people in this school never saw my humanity. Unlike the other places I had been, there was a curriculum for actual learning, and some people really wanted me to learn.

Another thing that did not go well: at the time, the school district had agreed to pay for the tuition and for an aide, someone who could learn how to facilitate, someone who would provide me with the supports I needed to learn, and to show I was learning.

The school however, refused to hire the aide. They even rejected the money available for it. The school refused to provide an accommodation needed for me to be able to learn, and show them that I was learning.

Good things happened there too.

For the first time in my life as a student, I had a science class, I had a history class, and I had a lot of literature. I listened to teachers explaining things like magma, or explaining the history of India. I heard about Shakespeare. It was a modified curriculum but whatever subject we were learning was the same a non-disabled student would learn. The information we received was the correct information.

I was in the classroom for the first part of the day. Because I didn't have an aide, I never got the support I needed to participate and ask questions. A lot of people in that school did not believe I could type, and they didn't make any effort to work with me. I still liked the classes. My brain absorbed everything, and I kept learning.

The second part of the day I spent outdoors, doing work that they called "land work." I had an aide then, but not for typing. The language used was that I needed one on one for land work and it had to be someone who could "handle me." Again, I was the "difficult" one.

Also ableist was the perception that I would never be able to show excellence in academic learning, so I had to learn some "skill" like picking up sticks, or carrying stones.

I liked it though. It was good to be outdoors—most of the time. Winters were hard. I did learn and I liked the movement. Some of the people who were assisting me were nice and I think they really liked me (at least they seemed to be ok spending a few hours with me).

Most of them were from different countries and spoke different languages. When they interacted with each other and spoke English, I could listen to the conversation and learn a little bit about their countries. It was a little like having friends just a little older than me, even if I wasn't included in the conversation. Today I see the ableism in the way they didn't really address me but at the time I was mostly ok, maybe because just being able to finally learn something filled me with satisfaction.

Reclaiming My Place in the World

Then, for the first time in a long time, someone believed in me. She was my teacher, she wanted to listen to me, and she took the time to type with me. I was, eventually, able to write poetry when working with her. Poetry is sometimes easier to type because I can convey a message with fewer words, and through a free style.

That was a good year. My parents even got me an AAC (Assistive and Augmentative Communication) device. It was a Dynavox, which I could use to type pre-recorded messages like greetings and simple requests (like "I'm hungry," or "I need some rest"). I could also use it to type letters and form words, just like I do today on an iPad, a computer or a letter board.

The sad part: due to personal reasons, that teacher had to leave in the following year. My Dynavox got lost—later found, but not working—and I was again silenced. At least I still had real classes. And I had more access to literary works, ending up with "The Barber of Seville," which we performed on "graduation" day.

I was 17. As I said, many in that school didn't want me there, so when I first arrived there they placed me with a class of older students, maybe hoping that I would finish the grades and leave soon. Because it was a "Special School" and because of the law, I would be considered a student until I turned 22 years old but they didn't expect me to stay there that long.

So, my actual learning life was about to end, after only two and a half years. I would probably have to go back to my hometown, and because the education situation there had not improved, I would probably have to move to a group home, be sent to "adult day programs" during the day. Or I would have to live with my parents, who had to work, and have someone keeping me company during the day.

Luckily, some people in that school wanted to try a new program, that they called "Transition." It was supposed to be like a life skills period of transition into adult life as a disabled person. It would be better than going back home because I already knew the place, people knew me, I was mostly happy there. With three other students, I was allowed to stay and be part of that new program.

That transition year would have been very boring if not for the fact that I met the person who would become my best friend. She was a volunteer in the school, and she was my caregiver. We have been together ever since.

My days were supposed to be filled with vocational training but I ended up being taken from place to place without any real instruction. Besides having a body that does not respond to the brain commands in a typical way—sometimes it doesn't respond at all—I also have physical disabilities that make it impossible for me to do certain things without a lot of help. The program didn't have enough people to assist me—and the other three disabled people.

There wasn't any formal continuing education either and I missed school. The good thing was that my new friend really wanted to know me and to learn my method of changing communication. So I taught her.

She asked some people and started to support my hand and wrist, letting me point to letters. She had never heard of FC, and wasn't a trained facilitator. Later, she would get the training and understand better the process. But in the beginning, she was simply presuming my competence. Maybe she was curious. She says that she was very skeptical of her ability to be a facilitator but never doubted that I could type my thoughts. Somehow, she noticed that communication doesn't always need words. The eyes, the body, how we react, these are also ways to communicate.

We practiced everyday—when we were together because she was with the younger students most of the time. In the beginning, I could not form any words. It takes time to build a relationship. It also took her some time to learn how to give me the right amount of resistance (like the FC training requires). Since we lived in the same house, and she was my main personal assistant, we became closer. We liked each other's souls, I guess.

Then, I was able to type a few words. Later, I typed a sentence. And then we were communicating—still short statements and answers that were not too complex. That summer she visited me. I already knew that we would be together again the next year, and that the program was going to expand and become better. It did, and I was going to be able to show everyone all that I had learned. It was also the year when I could explore my curiosity and learn more about all the things I wanted.

The next couple of years I was able to ask questions and give my opinion on many subjects. For the first time in my life I was reading newspapers and forming my own opinions on current events. We could discuss what was happening in the world, check the entertainment section of the paper, and even if I didn't care much about sports, we would read that too. With new friends to share my views with, it felt like I was part of the world.

I had a lot to catch up on, though. My eagerness to learn only grew. The more I read, the more I wanted to know, to research things that were mentioned in articles and that I had never studied. My friend, and sometimes other friends, would talk to me in the evening, and sometimes I would ask more questions. Most of the time though, I would just go to bed and let all the information find its place in my brain.

I was lucky. I was finally being heard, and I wasn't being ignored.

This all happened as I was becoming an adult and my curiosity has not diminished. I am still learning, changing some of my views, growing.

Since that first year of feeling like part of the world, I started reclaiming my place in it. I moved to a different city, in a different state, and my life expanded. I met new people who were interested in listening to my words, I joined poetry writing classes, and I started typing about my life—in verse.

As I paid more attention to world events, I started to pay attention to how people were talking about Autistics, like me. I didn't like what I saw. I didn't like the fear mongering and the false assumptions. So I taught myself to write in prose, to write letters to the newspapers, to write articles about what it means to be me.

Some people suggested that I should take GED classes, get a real diploma and then go to college. But that's not what I want. There are too many things that I cannot control and that are against me. My many disabilities would also make it hard for me to keep up. I am also happy with the way I learn and experience things. It works for me.

Social media is a way for me to learn—despite what I call "the fake news phenomenon." Because I really want to learn, I research what I read. I expand my knowledge by listening to audio books about different subjects. I can, if I have the energy, debate issues online. I can give my expert view, as a disabled person, on disability issues. After so many years of being ignored and silenced, I want my voice to be heard.

What I have learned the most, what I have to learn even more, and what I am most proud of knowing, is the history and the continuing fight for disability rights. I know what I know because I have been reading what other disabled people write.

I know what I know because I meet, in real life and online, other disabled people.

I learned that there is a word for how disabled people are (mis)-treated: ableism.

I also learned that I had a lot of internalized ableism, the urge to see myself as others saw me: as a lesser human being.

Then I had to unlearn ableism, and my online friends helped me with that too.

I learned about activism.
I became an activist.
I read.
I ask questions.
I debate.
I form opinions.
I question assumptions.
I question myself.
Then I learn some more.

It took me a long time to be able to start learning. I had to go through years of non-learning, because of the presumption of incompetence, before I was lucky enough to meet people who simply assumed I could absorb information and have thoughts.

It should not have been this complicated if the schools, teachers, therapists and doctors had stepped out of their bubble and had seen me.

Access.

Support.

Respect.

Every student needs these to be able to learn.

Every non-speaking student needs these to be able to learn.

SECTION 2

A Movement Toward Full Inclusion

4

Not Talking Is Not the Same as Not Thinking

Ido Kedar

Ido Kedar is a twenty-three year old author, blogger and autism advocate. He began learning to type via letter board and later keyboard and iPad when he was approximately seven years old. By middle school he was a fully included general education student. Between the ages of twelve and fifteen he completed his first book, Ido in Autismland: Climbing Out of Autism's Silent Prison. *This book, written in journal form, is a series of essays that attempts to explain autism from the inside out and challenges many of the prominent theories about autism. His book is used in many university courses. Ido's second book,* In Two Worlds *(2018) is a novel about a nonspeaking autistic boy named Anthony. Through the power of fiction, it offers the reader an unprecedented insider's view into the experience of living life in silence and into the two worlds of autism, the internal sensory world and the external world of nonstop therapy and endless misunderstandings. With humor and sensitivity it describes Anthony's journey to communication. It is a journey much like that undertaken by many of the contributors to this book. Ido blogs at www.idoinautismland.com.*

My Story

My formal education began shortly after I turned three years old with a teaching method known as applied behavior analysis, or ABA. ABA is highly recommended to parents of young autistic children by physicians and other experts. They encourage parents to obtain as many hours as possible of this popular behavior modification treatment for their young children. The ideal is forty hours weekly for toddlers to maximize neuroplasticity and take advantage of the so-called "window of opportunity," which attempts to change an autistic brain into a more neuro-typical one. It is often home-based and teaches through drills, or discrete trials, which are designed to incrementally teach the autistic child the meaning of basic words, emotions and other concepts typical children acquire without instruction.

My lessons were so rudimentary, it was mind numbing. The assumption was that I understood nothing, had no understanding of feelings, didn't differentiate people, and needed to be taught in the most basic way. I heard baby talk only, the word "the" was eliminated, as were possessives ("Touch nose!" "Go car!" "Brush teeth!") and the behaviorists simplified language to avoid using complete sentences. All in all, the language they used was designed to help someone who didn't comprehend words. The problem for me was that my processing and understanding of speech was normal, even superior. My drills and lessons presumed that I had the opposite problem of my real situation. In fact, my greatest deficit has always been motor. To be taught incorrectly for my real needs was not only boring and frustrating, it also frightened me that my true intelligence would go undiscovered because my body behaved so stupidly. This made for a rough childhood. I received forty hours of home-based ABA therapy weekly until I started school. After that, my ABA sessions continued, though for fewer hours on weekends and after school. I also received speech therapy, occupational therapy and other therapies. Yet despite all these interventions, I was still expressively limited to only my most basic needs and wants.

I also experienced what I can only describe as a weekly humiliation, in the form of ABA supervision, during which I performed my drills before the entire team who worked with me. Then my deficits and mistakes were discussed in front of me. This was again due to the incorrect assumption that I did not understand the discussion and it added shame and anger to my frustration. I had to endure this situation for five years. I am sorry if I offend ABA fans with my description because I know that ABA has been helpful for some people, but it is essential that people also understand the experience of a recipient of this widely used method of instruction who had less success with its methods. There are many of us.

Most theories about severe autism that are used today by educators and other professionals are based on the belief that severe nonverbal autism is a learning problem with receptive and expressive language delay, low cognitive capacity, concrete thinking, lack of humor, lack of empathy, lack of theory of mind, and often even an absence in basic awareness of the surrounding world. The expressionless faces, difficulty making eye contact, the sometimes bizarre looking self-stimulatory behavior, and the inability to speak can make intelligent people appear not to be. As a person with autism, this is deeply frustrating. Because of my outer presentation, strangers may incorrectly assume I need simplified talk. I cannot stop my neurological forces from camouflaging my real essence. Inside there is a person who thinks, feels, jokes, and has a lot to say. On the outside, people see my odd movements.

Once I started elementary school I attended a self-contained autism class on a regular campus. I envied the normal kids in every way. I wanted to play sports at recess, I wanted to joke with the kids and I wanted to learn in school, like they did. But I had no means to communicate or play like typical kids because of my severe motor apraxia. Apraxia robbed me of the ability to gesture communicatively, to handwrite independently, to show my emotions with the correct facial affect at will, to play sports and games at recess and, of course, it robbed me of the ability to speak. I was bored in remedial lessons and longing to learn, but I stagnated in my class. Mostly I passed the time in my internal sensory world because my reality felt pointless. I was locked inside my own body and feared I would be trapped like this forever.

A Turning Point

I have a loving family and that was my saving grace. Many times my mother suspected I understood things but that I couldn't show it. My school performance, speech therapy and ABA drills proved otherwise because they concentrated on speaking, something I really could not get my body to do. This left me with a communication repertoire of only a small number of spoken words which few people could understand because of my verbal apraxia, or a primitive pictogram system which was limited only to the most basic needs and wants. It was pure lucky chance that started my liberation to real communication when I was seven.

My motor skills are impaired, as I've described. My hands fumble and I've written that they feel like baseball gloves. Between the motor, neural processing and initiation challenges, independent handwriting was something I simply could not do as a child. At the time, I needed tactile support to be able to hang onto my pencil and scratch out letters. My mom and I worked in this way on my birthday party invitations. She would tell me the letter I needed to write, and with her helping to support my hand, I followed her instructions. As we were working on the invitations she realized she had forgotten to include a word and said aloud what she wanted me to write. Before she could say each letter out loud for me to write down, my own hand began to move and spell the word, with her hand still over mine, supporting it. She immediately realized what was happening, that I was understanding language and spelling without her instructions. Many times professionals had warned against the possibility of "inadvertently" giving the answers, as if any support or prompt is proof that the autistic person had no intellectual input in the answer. In fact, I am certain, if my mother had not supported my hand that day, I would never have been able to get my hand to move in the way I needed it to. That is because when I was seven I could not feel my body's position in space and my fumbling hand lacked the necessary motor control to hand write without support. Pressure or touch informed my body of its boundaries and her hand helped me to hold onto my pen in order to write the desired letters.

To make sure of what she was seeing, she had me add in more and more words onto the invitations without spelling the words out for me and each time she felt my hand moving under hers, writing it down correctly. I wrote messily, but I wrote. Finally we stopped working on the invitations because she had the proof she needed. She opened a notebook and in this way we had a conversation, our first. It was very emotional for both of us. She knew it had not been her moving me. She knew she had merely supported the pen in my hand. I knew that someone finally understood that I could read and spell, and most importantly, to think and understand. It was a big moment that began the huge change that eventually came to my life, but it wasn't simple or linear because, for quite a while, we couldn't convince anyone else that I was really communicating.

If you know my mom, she is the last person to live in a fantasy world. It is hard to find anyone more practical, yet everyone thought she had totally flipped. She had discovered that her mute, locked-in, strangely behaving son could understand normally, could think, feel and longed for a normal life, and all she got from the professionals was a kind of, "There, there," sympathetic eye roll and condescending pat on the shoulder. In fact, the educators and ABA team had no ability to see beyond their theories and recognize that I really was communicating. They dismissed what I wrote as inconsistent with their data and acted as if my mother was deranged for believing it. I have to say that this created a lot of stress for me. I was seven years old and thrilled to be communicating at last after years of forced silence, but to then be doubted by my team of professionals hurt me deeply at the time. I naively hoped that they would see my efforts and be happy for me, but I discovered instead that they viewed my communicating as impossible, and so they chose to ignore it. I'll admit that my early attempts at communication were far from fully independent, so a skeptical response was reasonable. But outright rejection was not. I was like a kid beginning to learn to ride a two-wheel bicycle, and still needed help from someone to stay upright, but they seemed to believe I should be able to do the equivalent of mountain biking on my own right from the start. Obviously a motor impaired autistic kid needs some help initially in learning to move the necessary way to communicate. It's irrational to expect full mastery in independent communication instantaneously, yet that is what they appeared to demand. I believe that they are not mean people but their closed-minded attitudes felt mean to a little autistic boy desperately trying to be heard and recognized as intelligent for the first time in his life.

The majority of my team of autism professionals absolutely did not understand a neurological system like mine. They firmly believed that if I received support of any kind in communication, it indicated that I lacked a skill, and worse, was being controlled. My father is a scientist and researcher and he insisted that we must find a way to enable me to communicate without any tactile support so that no one would doubt it was me expressing my own thoughts. Luckily, one psychiatrist we knew had heard of Tito and Soma Mukhopadhyay who had just moved to the United States from India. Tito was also severely autistic but his mother had taught him to communicate by typing and handwriting, which he did independently. He had been studied at UC San Francisco by a team of researchers who saw that he was the real deal, a severely autistic thinker who understood and communicated on his own. Quickly, therefore, he had to be disavowed by many professionals, like several of those who worked with me did, as being "one in a million," or "not really autistic." The ideal response would have been for professionals to consider whether Tito's successes and the way his mother taught him could be replicated in other nonspeaking autistic people, but because he was "one in a million," or "misdiagnosed," they simply continued to teach the exact way they always did.

I was one of the lucky kids who got to work with Soma when she was just starting out. In many ways, unfortunately, I was nearly alone in my venture. I knew no other autistic kids who typed at that time. I had to forge my own path without role models, but on the other hand, I was lucky beyond luck that I had been given this opportunity. I met Soma in her home and she taught me the way she had taught Tito, using age appropriate lessons and helping me to focus and point accurately to letters on a letter board while giving me verbal prompts to remind me to look, scan, and touch accurately. It was difficult, but in this way I began to learn how to communicate my own ideas without any tactile support. It was not what is referred to as facilitated communication because she didn't hold or touch my pointing arm, but sometimes she put a hand on my leg if I seemed restless or needed grounding and if I froze she sometimes helped me to get started by moving my hand to the first letter of an answer. Then I'd proceed with the rest of the spelled sentence on my own.

My teacher and ABA supervisor, however, observed me in an early lesson and believed I could somehow read letters telepathically through Soma's hand on my leg or by anticipating all the letters of the words in the sentence she helped me start by putting my hand on a single first letter. Essentially, she was viewed as being my puppeteer and my efforts and accomplishments were dismissed.

This is pretty infuriating to remember. Here is a trapped young kid finally making his first steps at communicating his ideas and his esteemed experts brush it aside as a myth from the very start. I had more anger than I like to remember about that. I truly felt betrayed by the people who had always seemed so invested in my success. I realized that in order to convince them, I would have to achieve goals using only their methods, one flashcard at a time. However, it was necessary to persevere, and we did. It took years, not overnight, to reach the level of proficiency I now have with typing in which I type alone on a tablet.

If I had not been taught how to control my hand enough to type with my index finger, first on a letter board, later on a keyboard or iPad, my ideas, jokes and thoughts would have been known only to myself. This is how it is for thousands of people with autism who cannot communicate. As I have described, their outside appearance is compromised by strange compulsive movements like hand-flapping, waving strings, carrying random objects around, pacing, impulsive actions and odd vocalizations, and beyond that they may have difficulty organizing their body to follow directions to simple tasks or questions, adding to the impression that they are intellectually delayed. The challenge for professionals, like those who worked with me when I was young, is to imagine that in spite of a person having these very visible external challenges, for many, these behaviors have nothing to do with intelligence but rather are due to a disconnect between the brain systems responsible for thought and movement.

It was a difficult journey for me to escape autism education. When you have the combination of a weirdly moving body, impulsive actions, lack of verbal speech and are a student in a remedial autism class, Individualized Education Program (IEP) committees tend to assume you lack the intellectual ability to learn standard curriculum. Several years after I had started communicating, my parents still had to bring films of me typing and a private educational psychology evaluation proving I was intelligent to try to convince a skeptical IEP committee that I deserved a chance to learn more than preschool curriculum. There was a woman from the school's augmentative communication department who came to the IEP and she alone was easily able to observe in the films how I was communicating by pointing to letters. Interestingly, she had worked for years with deaf students and was fluent in American Sign Language. She immediately argued to get me out of my "low functioning" autism class. That was when I was ten.

They decided to place me in a "high functioning" autism class where all the children spoke but required modified lessons. This was a difficult transition because I had to get used to a long day of sitting quietly. In fact, academics was the easy part. The hard part was my restless motor system, made worse by the slow pace of instruction. The skeptical teacher and administrators made me feel unwelcome. I felt very lonely there. For these reasons, when I started middle school the next year, I decided to go to my local middle school. I returned to a "low functioning" autism class with my former classmates but I was also included in two regular classes, science and math, with no academic modification. Then I spent the rest of the day in the autism room doing my own work. The school agreed that if I did well I would be mainstreamed in more subjects. I had a one-on-one aide who functioned as my scribe, communication support, and as my behavior support person.

Each year, as I became more accustomed to sitting for longer periods quietly in a class, my middle school included me in more regular classes. By the eighth grade the school determined that I was a fulltime general education student and no longer part of the autism or special education program at all. When I graduated middle school, I went to a regular high school, where I took honors and advanced placement classes. I performed well academically and I even graduated with honors, ranked fourth in my class. This was all thanks to my learning to communicate by pointing to letters and typing.

What My Future Holds

I currently study math and science and enjoy my hobbies of cooking and hiking. I work as an author and advocate. I wrote my first book, *Ido in Autismland: Climbing Out of Autism's Silent Prison*, when I was in middle school and early high school, between the ages of twelve and fifteen. It was my goal to change the way people looked at non-speaking autism. I wrote about my emotions living with autism. I described autism symptoms. I addressed sensory processing issues, motor issues, impulsivity, self-stimulatory behavior, and the many neurological and behavioral challenges I face. I also wrote about my early life and education. My deepest wish was to help parents look beyond the external traps and realize that their child might potentially be able to learn normally. My book has surpassed my hopes in reaching parents and professionals all over the world to change the paradigm in which they view autism. It has been translated into other languages and has been assigned in university classes. It has changed lives and I am proud to have helped my silent peers and their loved ones by writing it. My blog, www.idoinautismland.com, is a kind of extension of the book and serves as a forum for people to learn and understand more about autism.

My second book, *In Two Worlds,* a novel, may be the first fictional book written by a person with nonspeaking autism. But this novelty is not the reason I wrote it. It is a book I am immensely proud of, well-reviewed on its own merit, and one that enables the reader to understand nonspeaking autism and the experience of families living with it in a way that only fiction can provide. It allows the reader to enter the thoughts and heart of the hero, Anthony, to understand his inner sensory world and the outer world of therapeutic treatments, family, and school teachers and administrators, who try to help, but do not understand the true nature of his challenges.

The first half of the novel takes the reader deeply into his silent world. In the second half, we follow him as this world begins to open when at the age of sixteen he finally learns to communicate by pointing to letters. But like many of us, he also encounters a less than enthusiastic response by his professional team.

Through my writing, teaching and advocacy, my hope has been to prompt professionals, researchers, parents and others to reconsider current autism treatment trends and to listen to the real experiences of people with autism. It is my dream that more and more severely autistic people will be taught to be able to express their thoughts and ideas and to obtain a more appropriate education for their true intellectual needs.

Recommendations

Here are some recommendations for schools, therapists, and families to consider.

Provide Access to Communication

Communication is a basic, innate human need and humans, even those with autism, have an innate capacity for understanding and expressing language. The educators and many professionals I worked with before I could type were limited by their low expectations of their students. Applying the same words they used to describe their students, I could describe them as being resistant to new ideas, resistant to change, and rigid and concrete in visualizing the possibility of their students having greater potential. The assumption that people with severe autism all have impaired thinking has resulted in the underestimating of the true abilities of thousands of individuals, lack of adequate educational opportunities, isolation, loneliness, boredom, frustration, hopelessness, and a life of entrapment within one's own body. This price is too high.

My expressive communication skills, though far from being like that of a neuro-typical person, have improved a great deal from when I was a child because I can type now on a letter board, keyboard, or iPad. Each year my motor system becomes more under my own control. As I mentioned, I communicate alone by one-finger typing and that is the best I can hope for. Ten-finger typing is out of reach. Still, my one finger typing or pointing to letters has been the difference between stagnation in a low remedial autism program and receiving a general education. It is the difference between being thought to be a concrete thinker and being known to be funny, compassionate and intelligent. My one finger typing is the equivalent of sign language to a deaf person. It is my modality of communication and it gives me access to the world and control over my life.

I recommend that you observe people who have successfully taught typing to communicate to nonspeaking or limited speaking autistic people. Notice if their students progress and become increasingly independent in their communication. This success is something worth exploring. It is also important to listen to those people with autism who have broken through their silence who are now able to describe their experiences. We offer insights from the inside. This is valuable because, as I've described, simply observing our outside behavior may be misleading and may result in incorrect assumptions and theories. Treatments can go astray as a result.

Acknowledge and Address the Mind-Body Disconnect

As I stated earlier, when I was young my body rarely obeyed my mind. If I wanted to say no, my mouth said yes. If I wanted to say yes, my mouth said no. This kind of frustrating experience happened often because of the unreliability of my verbal responses and my inadequate control over my body. I had similar unreliability with my gross motor system. For example, if I wanted to point to a flashcard in an ABA drill my hand often went to the wrong card against my mind's wishes, as if my body had a mind of its own. My mind would tell me to walk to one room but my feet would insist on taking me to another. My mind wanted to open the car window. My hand repeatedly went to the door. My hands could not count the right number of straws or forks, though my mind knew the right number. These frustrating experiences are like gambling by rolling dice. My dice might land on my body not listening to me at all, or perhaps it would land on enabling me to do an action partially and inadequately, or perhaps it would land me on another neurological tangent altogether in self-stimulatory movements, or if I was lucky, the dice might land on enabling me to do exactly what I wished to do. The result is that people assume you don't understand language. Without communication, your locked in body does not enable you to prove otherwise.

In my book, *Ido in Autismland; Climbing Out of Autism's Silent Prison*, I describe how when I was small we visited relatives and my mother instructed me to give my aunt a bouquet of flowers. The problem was that my aunt was behind me and my other relatives were in front of me. What does a kid like me who cannot initiate a search motorically do? I gave the flowers to the person I saw standing in front of me, knowing it was not my aunt and knowing people would assume I either didn't understand the meaning of the command or I couldn't tell one relative from another. If I grabbed the wrong can from the shelf after being instructed to get an item, it was not because I lacked the knowledge of what tuna fish was, it was because at that time I lacked the ability to search and scan. I still have difficulty adjusting my blankets in bed or even initiating the movement to get another blanket if I am cold. Does this mean I'm too stupid to identify how I feel? No, it means I can't get my body to do what I want it to do, when I want it to, with reliability and consistency. This is entrapment. It is not receptive and expressive language confusion, and most definitely not a lack of thought, emotions and awareness. In my opinion, this is like a paralysis of intentional responses, even though my body is moving. In contrast, when it comes to self-stimulatory behavior, I often cannot get my body to stop moving to its internal impulses though I may desperately want it to.

Because of this, it is unfair for professionals to assume they know what is in the mind of a person with nonspeaking autism simply because of what he shows externally. Again, if a person cannot speak, cannot control his facial muscles to express his feelings at will, cannot gesture, and cannot hold a pencil to write, how can this person prove that he understands? Why is it commonly assumed that a person with these challenges has cognitive delay when everything I mentioned in the previous sentence can also be seen as an example of a motor issue?

Data, even accurate data, can be misleading. I have described my early experiences with ABA but I would like here to address the impact of data. When I performed my discrete trials my instructors took meticulous records regarding whether I pointed to the right card or not or how many prompts I needed to perform a drill. They thought they were collecting data on my receptive understanding of language. They were not. I understood everything, as any other child my age would. The data they were collecting, though they did not know it, actually measured my poor ability at that time to get my hand to touch with accuracy the card I wanted, and did not reflect an accurate measure of how much I understood. My mind might be screaming, "Touch tree! Don't touch house!" and I would watch, like a spectator, as my hand went to the card my hand, not my brain, wanted. And down in the data book it would be marked that I had not yet mastered the concept of tree. My plea to neuro-researchers is that this is a neurological force that needs to be a focus of study.

Unlike Stephen Hawking who lost his motor control progressively as an adult, but who was widely recognized to be an intelligent person despite being unable to speak or control his hand, autistic children are born with their speech problem and motor challenges. If Stephen Hawking had been born with his communicative disability, would the experts have believed that he too didn't understand language and never taught him to use his assistive technology?

Since I believe my mind/body disconnect is a key to my odd movements and body apraxia, I have found that a vigorous exercise program focusing on strength, coordination and flexibility has helped me with my motor control tremendously, because the fitter I am physically, the more my body obeys my mind. It is possible for people with autism to get fit and strong. Exercise also helps with my emotional equilibrium and helps to reduce the constant anxiety that so many people with autism experience. I recommend that young children with autism work on real physical fitness early. We need smart fitness programs more than we do swings.

Train Aides and Communication Partners

I want to discuss the importance of having a good aide. It is impossible to overstate the harm an incompetent aide can make in upsetting a fragile neural system already working at peak overload to cope with the many noises, crowds, and visually overwhelming scenes of a typical school. I have had many talented and competent support people who had the ability to understand me behaviorally, who could easily follow my communication pointing to letters, had the ability to support me in class in terms of my restlessness, as well as serve as a scribe by writing down my in-class essays or in filling in the bubbles on tests for me. Our partnership was obvious. I did the brainwork. I wrote the essays and answered the questions and they wrote my ideas down for me because I lacked the fine motor ability to do that myself. When I answered questions on a letter board they spoke my words out loud. The ideal situation is a respectful partnership. An incompetent or uncaring aide can severely impact the success of a person with autism. An aide who is unable to communicate fluently with the autistic student undermines success at every level.

A Final Message

I have one more message to parents who wonder if their child can learn to type to communicate. Only the most determined parents will find out. If you are working with experts like those from my early life, they will limit your child in low expectations. They tell you that being impaired in body is being impaired in mind. They let you work on skills that barely progress and tell you that your child isn't advanced enough to write.

If you keep on listening to them they will keep low expectations for a lifetime. I know it is hard to be the parent who disagrees. I have watched many parents struggle against school district attitudes and professionals who could not see their children's potential. They went through a big hard slog. They also got their kids typing and into general education. More than anything else, the parents believed in the possibility that their child had more in them than they were told. Parents, you have to trust your gut. You see your kid all day in real life. They see a drill or a lesson, and those moments where the motor issues of severe autism are at their worst.

Professionals, I have a message for you too. I used to think you were all clueless and control freaks. This is not to say that people were not warm or kind because I liked my teachers as people but resented their attitude of certainty. If you work with autism, be prepared to accept that a degree in psychology or speech pathology or occupational therapy isn't giving an insight into more than symptoms. My brain and how it's impaired is a guessing game, even for neurologists, so I think the certainty that many practitioners have when it comes to autism is really puzzling. Being open-minded and admitting that the brain is vast and mysterious is required, in my opinion, by anyone who works with autistic people. Give people with autism the benefit of the doubt. Speak normally. Teach grade level lessons in school.

Finally, I have a message for people with autism who can't yet communicate, and I ask parents to read my essay to their kids: Have hope. More than anything, have determination. Life outside your head and stims is really worth striving for. I believe soon there will be too many people with autism who type to keep insisting we are one in a million. I am fighting for your freedom and so are others. Hang in there.

Relentless Hope

Samuel Capozzi

Samuel Capozzi is a senior at Cal State University Channel Islands who has autism and spells/types to communicate. He's considered non-speaking and non-writing, in other words, unable to write efficiently enough to keep up with the fast pace of higher education requirements. Samuel hopes to be a pioneer for others who face similar obstacles pursuing higher education and a career. He is honored to be on the board of Autism Society Ventura County and has the pleasure of being the first autistic board member. Samuel believes it is important to be present and included in decisions about and for the autism community as a non-speaking autistic—a vastly underrepresented voice. In 2015, he was awarded the Awesome in Autism "Individual of the Year" recognition and aspires to be a voice for the voiceless. Samuel enjoys sharing his experiences in various settings and through varied media. He thanks his incredible "sparkplug" of a mother, Kathryn, for her assistance in completing this chapter.

> *"Hope is a good thing, maybe the best of things. And no good thing ever dies."*—The Shawshank Redemption

Living with autism is lonely and arduous in ways most people could never understand. My journey as a non-speaking, non-writing autistic is as unique as any other person's story. Yet, you have picked this book up with the intent to broaden your understanding, and hopefully, appreciation for those of us, who like me, are nonspeaking but have a lot to say. By sharing my story and personal insights about autism, I aim to challenge your current ideas and perceptions about autistics. This essay offers you a peek into a life with autism, one in which hope evolves. This hope is rooted in a longing for access to communication and full participation in the community and in my own life. It begins with hardship that leads to expectant hope, then a life in which hope is realized, and, finally, a life bursting with relentless hope. This is my story of finding reliable, functional, true communication through spelling and typing to communicate. My story not only details my journey in finding said communication through spelling and typing to communicate; it also documents the ways in which access to communication made a profound impact on my educational pathway to higher education.

Expectant Hope

As a young child, I was very confused at times with the world around me and sometimes had difficulty making sense of daily life. My sensory processing system was haywire, and my senses were either entirely overwhelmed or just not responding well. I suppose as I became more self-aware it was even more confusing than during my childish ignorance. My mom once asked me when I knew I was autistic. Well, I knew I was different from a very young age, but I recall hearing that I "have autism" when I overheard conversations surrounding me in home behavioral therapy. I didn't know what that meant, but I guess in some way it explained some of my confusion—I "had" something that made me different. It would take years of listening and deduction to understand my diagnosis—moderate, non-speaking autism. Interestingly, now that I can communicate, I wonder if I still qualify for the "moderate" diagnosis? These labels, high-functioning, low-functioning, mild, moderate, and severe autism, seem misleading now that we are gaining a better understanding of autism. Am I now considered high functioning because I attend college? I can self-regulate and manage quite a bit of self-care which also may qualify as "high-functioning." However, I deal with impulsivity and high-anxiety, coupled with limited speech, which limits my ability to function independently out in the world—am I now low functioning? Yet, I know individuals who have Asperger's Syndrome that are highly impacted by autism and face significant challenges in all facets of life, and they are implicitly considered high-functioning. Yes, our understanding is still developing, but these terms seem relative to me now. Can I challenge you to reconsider these labels? I believe they perpetuate assumptions that are not always true and place significant limitations on those being labeled. Moderate autism or not, I am grateful my parents were so loving and confident in their parenting. My diagnosis never seemed to affect the joy and love I saw reflected in their eyes, again, offering me hope in the darkness.

My first memory of school, preschool actually, is not a warm one. Upon being diagnosed at the age of four, I began to receive services through our local public school system. I was enrolled in a preschool class for kids with autism. This memory surfaced when my mom asked me (later in life) a question about Harvard—-more about Harvard later! When my mom asked me how I knew about Harvard, I explained on my letter board, *When I was in school an adult in the classroom said that none of us would ever go there (Harvard), and I felt ashamed.* My mom inquired further, "So, how did you learn about Harvard?" Letter by letter, I spelled, *Every chance I had to hear about it, I listened.* This is an important point for educators who work with kids like me. I listened. My speech in preschool was limited and unreliable, but my hearing and comprehension were intact. In the end, it was a school psychologist who spoke those words within my earshot and that of my four-year-old peers. I must clarify, although my comprehension was intact, I didn't fully understand what she meant; however, I did realize that it was a "dis" (disrespectful). At four, I knew the spirit in which she said those words. Not a warm, fuzzy memory, right? Reflecting upon the school psychologist's words, I now realize they were both harmful and useful. They were harmful to the heart and soul of a confused little four-year-old, yet her words became a spring board that gave me drive to listen with deep intent *to truly understand* what was being said.

Even though the school psychologist may have been well meaning in dismissing us "poor little souls" from perceived difficult academic challenges, her mindset was dangerous. It was dangerously dismissive. You see, she was not only personally giving up on me, but she was also influencing the teachers and aides to do the same. I was four. Her dismissive mindset limited my current and future educational opportunities in my school curriculum placement. In contrast, when I was fully included in a regular education kindergarten class, my mom explained how my regular education teacher strongly exhorted the parent volunteers not to discuss the children, their learning, or their childish behavior amongst each other or anywhere for that matter. She explained that we were five years old and much would change over the next few years. She didn't want our reputations or future educational opportunities to be negatively impacted. This is one example of extremes in embracing educational ideology; it is hard not to feel like a second-class citizen as a student with a disability.

As the years went on, my parents advocated for me to be fully included in our neighborhood school during kindergarten and first grade. It was both good and bad. I enjoyed my classmates, but I was experiencing the frustration of a body that seemed to have a mind of its own and an increasing self-awareness that I was different than my peers. My early elementary years were filled with tears, meltdowns, physical suffering, and utter sadness due to lack of communication and extreme sensory dysregulation. Even as a child, I could see the strain this was having on my family. How hard life is for the autistic child— we feel and understand at a typical level but can't experience conversations to work life out like others. Frankly, we are often ignored entirely. Although not perfectly, my mom spoke to me in a way that was inclusive. Delightfully, she was right! I was comprehending everything another child my age would even if my body said otherwise. I can't emphasize enough how important it was to me that my parents spoke to me and included me; it was a lifeline of hope when most everyone else was content to ignore me or pacify me. Even though being fully involved with my peers was challenging due to my physically overwhelmed body, I learned a lot during that period. Days were long physically, but academically I couldn't get enough.

When I began to have reliable communication, my mom asked me when I learned to read. You see, before my communication breakthrough, I was "reading" (reading out loud) *Dick and Jane* books for 3–6 year olds at the age of sixteen—a dark time indeed. I told her that when I was in the doctor's office, I simply picked up a *Highlight's Magazine*, and I could read it. We figured out that I was seven years old at the time, and I was reading pretty fluently in my head. Between my parents and full inclusion, I learned to read at a typical time. I eventually explained that reading and reading out loud are two very different things. Please ponder this. In regular practice, students are taught to methodically track and read the words out loud. Although this may work with other autistic students, it was not helpful to me because I neither had reliable speech (output) nor could I orchestrate the many motor movements to demonstrate my fluency.

Because speech is a motor skill, not a cognitive skill, reading out loud becomes a huge obstacle for those of us who are non, unreliably, or minimally speaking. Do we have the verbal ability to learn to read at typical times? Yes, I believe most of us do. Almost certainly, as far as I can tell, many autistics have an incredible propensity for language and communication once given a reliable means to communicate. I often joke that I am "quite verbose" as I explain the difference between being non-speaking and being non-verbal. I can only speak for myself, but for me, reading is not only exhausting, but I don't track in a typical manner. I almost see the whole page at once and then isolate sentences. For this reason, I listen to my textbooks using Kurzweil© (software audio technology) or Audible©, someone may read to me (helps with focus), or someone will sit beside me and isolate a couple of sentences at a time (also helps with focus).

In first grade, the politics and bureaucracy of my autistic presence in a regular-education class began to unfold rapidly. Looking back, I realize I didn't have a reliable or functional means to communicate, and not only was this a non-issue for my school team but nothing was planned to address this vital need. Communication is a basic human right. Without functional communication, I was unable to describe my out of sync experience or demonstrate my knowledge or ask questions. Yet, I was expected to behave as if everything was fine. It wasn't. The frustrating thing about this period is the fact that I had a very good full-inclusion specialist on my team that dealt with their "hands being tied" by school personnel. Even though he had great ideas and methods about how to both include and support me, it often took weeks of bureaucracy to hear or implement his suggestions. At the time, I was grabbing and holding onto my aide's arms out of desperation to be understood and because my little-sapped body couldn't function. Since this was not going to be allowed by the principal of the school, I was pushed out, and he told my parents, "There are programs for kids like him." I was humiliated and began to act out even more. It was at this time that my parents felt like my hope and my soul were being crushed. They decided to pursue a home program for me. It was the right decision, and I am thankful my parents could always stir hope in my little broken-heart.

Hope Realized

Between the ages of eight and nineteen, I was immersed in a comprehensive homeschooling program. Life being homeschooled was a good fit for me, and I enjoyed the experience. Luckily, my parents kept me busy and continually pursued various therapies and interventions that would help me and enrich my life. That is, I received occupational therapy, speech therapy, equestrian therapy, auditory integration therapy, gymnastics, running-club, field trips, play dates, swimming lessons, nutritional and medical interventions, and a neurodevelopmental program (to name a few). Of course, this was in addition to my academic program!

I think it's important to describe where my communication was at this point—before I began to point to letters and spell to communicate. I have always had spoken language and used it regularly. Although I have speech, I was not then nor am I now a chatty fellow. Moreover, my speech is what I would call unreliable. I often said, and still say, things that are not what I mean. I call them blurts. It's a frustrating and daunting fact to live with unreliable speech. To be misunderstood is awful and disheartening. For example, I was "reading" (reading out loud) *Dick and Jane*, performing double-digit addition, and working far below grade level because I was unable to expressively communicate that I understood and learned at an average to above average level. To say that I was bored, exasperated, and depressed would be an anemic description of how I felt at that time. Although very remedial, I believe even this level of progress (expressively) just simply wouldn't have been sought had I remained in the stifled public school program in our local community. My family never stopped. My family believed I could continually make significant gains. My family found a way for me to have functional, reliable communication. Because of my speech, I never seemed to be a candidate for assistive technology or augmentative and alternative communication (AAC). Looking back on it now, I should have at least been evaluated while I was enrolled in the local public school system.

The turning point in my communication began during my home program. My mom watched a documentary called *A Mother's Courage* and saw families pursuing an academic intervention leading to communication called *Rapid Prompting Method©* created by Soma Mukhopadhyay. After my mom watched the documentary, she insisted my dad and I watch it too. The mom in this documentary came from Iceland to the U.S. in search of breakthrough therapies or interventions to help her young, autistic son. This mom visited all the think-tanks and high profile clinics addressing autism across the country. She travelled to Austin, Texas to visit Soma and watch her implement rapid prompting method with her clients. The mom's perceptions were challenged by observing non-speaking, young, autistic individuals spelling and typing to communicate.

My mom said that the look on this other mom's face, her complete shock and astonishment when her non-speaking son began to spell to communicate through this academic intervention, grabbed her complete attention. Mom explained to us that the sincerity of that moment sparked a renewed sense of hope for helping me to gain communication. Excitingly, something clicked for my parents, and we soon traveled to Texas to work with Soma in May 2012. My hope began to swell as I overheard them discussing the method and the trip. In the meantime, while waiting for our appointment, my mom read Soma's book(s) and started to implement some of the techniques with me. It became clear that this just might work. I was sixteen years old.

How do I describe my desire for true communication? How can I describe the moment my prayers were answered and my hope was realized? When I started to work with Soma, I knew right away that she was different than anyone I ever worked with before then. It was as if she saw right through me—at the very least she *saw me*. Initially, it scared me a little. As we began to work, I began to get emotional. Can this be it? Can I actually get my body to respond to her directions? To be frank, I was shocked myself that I was answering (expressively) her questions as simple as they were at first. I had to select between two choices by pointing, and then I would spell my answer on stencil boards with her support through verbal prompting and gestures. Delighted, I responded to questions about history, geography, and poetry—questions for a sixteen-year old's intellect. One of my warmest memories from this time was seeing my parents, eyes brimming with tears, hearts swelling out of their chests, mouths agape, as I spelled my little heart out. I began to taste true communication when I started spelling to communicate. As a family, we were stunned and our lives took on a new direction that day. As an individual, I began to feel hopeful in a whole new way, and life became much brighter. Sixteen years is a long time without functional communication. Can you imagine?

We returned home, and my mom began to work with me regularly. As far as I can tell, I had an unusually fast response learning to point to spell out my thoughts and responses. Although it may seem like a simple task, it is not for someone who has significant motor planning challenges and apraxia. It is difficult to get my mind and body on the same page, so using one finger to spell decreases the demand for motor planning and coordination. My first answer to an open-ended question from my mom was not only emotional, but it set off a whirlwind of communication and academic pursuits!

At that time, I was enrolled in a small private school that works on a hybrid model of homeschooling and part-time classwork and clubs. I was enrolling for fall classes when my mom asked me if I wanted to attend an English class. The class sounded a bit "heady" as they were going to be having literary roundtable discussions. Remember, *Dick and Jane* was what I was used to in my wheelhouse! After answering basic questions about the classes, I chose not to take the English class. With trepidation, mom asked me, "Can you tell me anything about why you don't want to be in this class, even one word?" Incredibly, I managed to spell out, "I am scared because I am autistic." Mom wet a towel with tears. I let out my own internal tears as well. I decided not to take this English class but ended up enrolling in lower level classes to build my skills and stamina with spelling to communicate through academics and adjust to being in a classroom setting. Eventually, I attended grade level and honor classes which I loved. To say that my hope was realized in May of 2012 would be an understatement. The door to reliable, functional communication had just swung wide open.

Hope Anticipated

As I made my way through high school with reliable communication with the support of a communication partner via the use of a laminated letter-board and iPad, my whole world changed. I now had a voice. I now had a voice in my own life. I now had a voice that was respected and even admired. It was surreal—even shocking. Although this is the case for those who know and love me, as a society, we have a long way to go to have a more inclusive, aware, and accepting climate for all autistics, but especially those who are non-speaking. Because I am well acquainted with living life both ways, it is my passion to both advocate for autistics and educate others about misconceptions, misunderstandings, and myths about us.

Once I could communicate reliably, I had the opportunity to be fully included in my high school and participate in leadership opportunities. This includes taking the National Latin Exam with my peers twice; acting as my school's World-Champion Mock Trial team Journalist; taking the SAT with accommodations; graduating with honors; contributing to a blog on *Joni and Friends* website; being accepted at all three universities where I applied; receiving healthy scholarship offers; speaking at conferences and seminars; being voted Individual of The Year by the Autism Society Ventura County; acting as Grand Marshal for Aut2Run charity race; attending a four-year university as a freshman and maintaining an "A" average; being the first nonspeaking student enrolled at my campus; being invited to be a member of a National Honor Society—Gamma Beta Phi; becoming a member of the national Political Science Honorary Society, Alpha Eta Phi chapter of Pi Sigma Alpha; being featured in several local newspaper articles, being chosen for a paid fellowship with the Self-Advocacy Resource and Technical Assistance Center (SARTAC); becoming an intern with the Autism and Communication Center at Cal Lutheran University; co-teaching with a speech-language pathologist to professionals learning to teach spelling to communicate; representing my local county on Capitol Hill; co-authoring a disability advocacy blog post with one of my professors, and writing an essay for this book. It's important to know this list is not to boast, *instead it's a list to demonstrate potential*. Can you see all of the wasted potential had I not found a reliable means to communicate—a voice? Can you see the wasted potential, the unknown brilliance of the many non-speaking autistics in our communities? More importantly, can you see the violation and injustice of being denied our fundamental human right and need to communicate? We should all hope for more.

I listed many accomplishments that don't *even* take into consideration the simple yet essential need to connect with others. We have feelings, emotions, and so much to offer those in our circles, to the conversation, and to society at large. It is my hope that these truths become better understood and that I may have a role in the process. It is my calling. It is my hope that you will grasp these truths and adopt a proactive role in the process of changing societal assumptions as well.

As the first non-speaking, non-writing student at Cal State Channel Islands University, I believe I am already advocating and educating simply by my presence. The mere fact that I am a full-time student excelling in my coursework (with the proper accommodations) is educating everyone I encounter on and off campus. What is my presence saying? *It can be done.* Again, with the right attitude and proper, meaningful, accommodations a student like me is successfully accessing higher education. Although not every person with autism can attend university, or may simply have no desire to, many could and should be given the opportunity if they so desire.

At this writing, I just completed the first semester of my fourth year at CSUCI. How can I communicate the satisfaction in making that statement? As I walk this path, I am becoming more aware of how exceptional my college is and how vital this is to my success as a nonspeaking, non-writing, autistic student. Although I am accessing higher education through the Americans with Disabilities Act (ADA) and Section 504 of the Rehabilitation Act, I am realizing not all campus services for students with disabilities are equal. Fortunately, my campus has a strong program led by intelligent, caring, educated professionals. As such, this affords me with comprehensive support and access to a variety of appropriate accommodations that contribute to my success accessing higher education.

Currently, although this list is not exhaustive, I receive extended time for exams, a quiet room if necessary, a notetaker, audio-versions of my textbooks, priority registration, access to my communication partner, access to my assistive technology (AT), and I meet with my professors in advance. With these accommodations and supports I am not only learning so much, but I am also earning top marks. Again, it is not a cognitive issue for me instead it is a motor issue, and I believe this is true for many of my peers with autism. Another thing that I do at the beginning of each semester is provide my professors with a One-Page Profile that contains information about me such as what is important to me, what is helpful, and other things I would like them to know. Being non-speaking is not the same thing as being non-thinking. Why do we equate these two things?

Upon considering my overall experience as a successful college student, it simply wouldn't be possible without my mom who goes above and beyond what most parents will or can do. I am concerned about this as an overarching obstacle for my marginalized, misunderstood peers. It shouldn't be this way. You see, it has become clear to me that I sit at an intersection of disability and privilege. Is my story of success as a non-speaking autistic, college student exceptional and even somewhat shocking? Yes, but it must be said, I have educated/intelligent, articulate, parents with means and access to resources and people (social capital) that have decidedly helped me along this successful path. It did not happen naturally. It was and is a great deal of hard work. The inequity to accessing higher education for autistics is still a harsh reality and has a whole life of its own!

Also, it seems many things need to be considered before every and any autistic individual, non-speaking or not, considers attending college. Are they ready socially, emotionally, physically? This is not to say "things" will look "normal," or even that the goal should be normalcy, but these areas still need to considered. More importantly, just because these areas may not look "normal" or typical certainly should not exclude someone with autism from higher education or otherwise. During my studies and in my life, I have learned that a strong transition plan (beginning as early as possible), a strong, motivated, equipped transition team, and significant professional collaboration is a big part of the solution for success with autistic students hopeful to attend college and other post-secondary programs. And although this wasn't my exact experience, it still seems highly important to consider moving forward as the "autism-boomers" all seem to have recently completed K–12 or will.

As a successful university student, I am approached by parents and professionals with questions about my experience. They are coming with children as young as nine years old. Consequently, this has caused me to consider what advice or information I can share with them. I wrote a research paper about what seems to be working and important for successful transition into college and other postsecondary programs. Again, the primary things were the strong transition plan, team, and professional collaboration. As I stated earlier, my journey to higher education is as most pioneering journeys—unique! As we learn what is and is not working, it is my hope that my experience(s) along with others' will inform professionals, individuals with autism, and their families about how to address some of the significant challenges. If I had to give some advice, I would encourage parents and professionals to be certain attending college or any other postsecondary program is the autistic individual's goal not their own. Because of difficulty with self-regulation, overriding intense sensory dysregulation, and dealing with impulsivity are challenging (to say the least), the person needs to want to be there— to drive their own program and life. I do understand the excitement the *simple possibility* brings to those who know and love someone with autism, I do. But they need to be in charge.

Finally, as I mature and pursue my goals, I aspire to study law. Of course, this isn't something I would have dared dream about before 2012—but, now I am hopeful that I can achieve this lofty goal. Speaking of law school, now for the story about Harvard! At the beginning of my communication breakthrough, I expressed my desire to study law and explained how I heard about Harvard. My flabbergasted mom probed, "Do you want to go there to prove someone wrong or make a point?" I explained, "Life is so short, and I have a passion to help people with special needs. God has put it on my heart, and it will show His power." Yes, I will probably be the first nonspeaking, non-writing student to apply to law school; however, I hope not to be the last. I *must* follow my calling, and I am so thankful I can. And, although Harvard is the dream, practically speaking, I will probably go somewhere near home. My friend and mentor, Joni Eareckson Tada, often quotes a line from *The Shawshank Redemption* movie that proclaims, "Hope is a good thing, maybe the best of things. And no good thing ever dies." It is my aim to pass along the lifesaving relentless hope—*maybe the best of things*—I have experienced to others as I share my journey from silence to soaring advocacy!

6

Letter by Letter

DILLAN BARMACHE

Dillan is a passionate, 20-year-old young man who communicates by spelling out his thoughts and ideas letter by letter on a letterboard or keyboard. Dillan is a college student studying psychology. Over the past few years, Dillan has had the privilege of sharing his experience of autism at conferences, with students at universities and elementary schools, and through his Typing4Change blog and Facebook page, in the hope of shifting perceptions about autistic individuals. Dillan was honored to receive the HollyRod Autism Champion Award from the HollyRod Foundation and the Re-imagine Autism Award from the Autism Society of Los Angeles. In April of 2016, Dillan was featured in two films by Apple during Autism Acceptance Month—Dillan's Voice and Dillan's Path—with the message that every individual deserves to be truly seen and heard. Dillan could never have gotten through such an emotional effort like writing this chapter without his caring communication partners. "Deb and Jim, thank you always."

I am so ready to let the world know that they are all wrong about autism. Yes, I am autistic. It's a part of me. A hard way to be in this world with a certain perspective. Many people dread the idea that we could actually exist in many numbers, because no one visualizes us this way, with thinking minds intact. Having a voice leaves hard questions for people to answer. People do not want to think that they have been so wrong for so long, which makes it hard to really see me, and others like me. Day in and day out I deal with all of these challenges. Believe me, I get it why people have such a hard time with this. All I ask is that you try to have an open mind to ideas that defy existing ones. If our ideas about the world remain stagnant then we can never move beyond ignorance.

It's not enough to imagine we might exist. We are real to those who are forceful, and determined to fight against the existing belief that autism is a major, catastrophic mental deficit that exists in all of us without a voice. There are so many of us, and it's time to listen to our message, include us in all of the decisions that must be made, and share our thoughts with the people that are there to support us in our lives. I know that it's a lot of work, but we all have the potential to make amazing progress together. Having someone fighting for your right to give you a voice is the greatest feeling that anyone could have. To march among these kinds of people is to me a great honor.

The first step to accepting the voices of autism into the conversation about our future is to understand the experience that we have inside of us. Our minds are in constant conflict with intention and impulse. We live with two minds.

My Two Heads

BOY WITH TWO HEADS

Once upon a time a boy had two heads. But the doctors did nothing with them. One head was smart, other head was autistic. People could not see the smart head. They only saw the autistic head. But the smart head heard and saw everyone. One day, the smart head was really tired of the autistic head, because that head had the same sound pattern for twenty minutes. Smart head could not think, so he had to fall asleep and waited for autistic head to calm down.—Dillan Barmache, age 11

I am totally autistic—hear that as the words out of my mind, not my mouth. Words that come from my mouth are often echoes of another person, which do not have the power of my intention. Other times, only in rare golden moments does my mouth actually speak my mind. In those cases, the thoughts continue on in my mind even as the words die, escaping into beastly noises.

Having my kind of autism is not going where you want to go or doing what you want to do. One second I can be sitting making toys line up, then animals in another place would call me, and I was off on a hunt to find them. All of it comes in intense flashes of impulse not from choices made. I am too lost in following the rote movements my body has learned in its muscle memory. People see the actions and hear the babbling, and they think I am driving my body in nonsense patterns with purpose and intent. It's the opposite. Having a mind body disconnect is like having a lost phone signal or a bad Internet connection. The thought of what I want to do never reaches my limbs intact. I desperately want to be in control of my body with intention and purpose. I so wish people would be able to understand that although I look and move in ways you would not expect from a person who is understanding everything around them, I am a thinking, feeling person just like you. Many autistics suffer from the same mind-body disconnect.

The autistic impulses that seem to take me away from the world can make it hard for anyone to know me. They become a barrier even to my close, loved family members. I am lost in my patterned movements even as I want to respond to their words or tell them my strong feelings for them. It is easy for them to look at me and think that I have no wish to speak with them. If my own family can assume I am lost to their world, think what a stranger might assume as I stare intently at the ceiling when they greet me. My intentions to connect with people are buried under the burden of the heavy weight of my autism. The desires and feelings to connect to my loved family stay hidden underneath, and only come to light in tiny moments where my intentional mind can be in control.

However, not everything about my autism is a burden to me. Autism is amazing in the way my reality is experienced. My sensory system is like a movie that doesn't play on the screen in a way you might think. You have no idea how important my sensory system has been for me. I may look like I'm not in this world, or tuned out like so many of you think, but what is really happening is that I am absorbed in the world around me. My mind keeps track of all the sensory information like a movie that I can manipulate. I am able to fast forward, slow down, and even pause the world. I have always enjoyed placing the world on pause and studying it in extraordinary detail.

I am sorry you don't get to experience autism, but I am happy that you do not have to deal with being made to think something is so wrong with you that you should not ever think that you deserve more out of life.

Before communication, my world was in total isolation. My family loved me, and I felt their love and wished I could speak to them and say, "I'm in here." They, more and more every day, saw autism acting in my place. Autism acting out my feelings of loneliness in the way I line up my animals, in the way I make my piles, in the way I scream, laugh or run away. Always autism acting in my place, not me. Not my mind that wanted to love back and to be included. It is hard to describe a world that is in total control of you. It is hard to describe how impossible it was to be always in prison. No words can fully explain it. My words fill in parts of an experience that I existed in; an experience that was totally overwhelming to my senses and in my emotions. I was in chains, made helpless by a sensory and emotional system that was faulty, and with the education system unwilling to recognize that I could live any other way, I was doomed to remain trapped.

The Voiceless Years

"Before, I only had my sounds and noises to try to be heard and understood. I tried to say what I really wanted—had to try even though it all came out as screams and laughter."

In elementary school, I was in an autistic class that for years showed me that I was far more set in my autistic mind than people could handle. The lessons being taught were pathetic and simple, but my sensory system was so overrun each second of every day that I could not respond in a demonstration of my understanding. I only had my connections with the items that called to my autistic mind to help me get through each day, like my plastic elephants. Yes, I even thought when I found the difference between my autistic mind and my regular mind that my life and education would be better, but things did not improve.

Being autistic affects my ability to make my movements intentional with my thoughts. Too many times I was asked to do the simplest things; gathering certain shapes, for example, being a common skill taught in such programs. But when I moved to sort, only autism controlled my hands. My mind could try all it wanted, but it was impossible. Finding myself in this hopeless place pushed me further into autism and almost killed my spirit.

Many days from 1st grade and long after were spent sorting the shapes on my desk. I was asked to find the diamond out of other shapes or attempt to keep all shapes in similar piles. They were big, easy wooden shapes too (baby ones!). They gave harder ones as the trials got easier for me. Damn, I hated shapes. Teachers decided that identifying and sorting shapes would be the academic goal I lived for. That was very insulting, so then going crazy was better. Each time I acted out it was assumed I had not understood the directions. I can't tell you enough how hard it was in those moments not to be able to reach for that diamond. Through each and every year, my moronic education demanded nothing of my capable mind.

Imagine that I am sitting at my desk and have a book in my hands. A little paper one called *Dan Sitting on a Rug*, with little, very easy words, the kind that you do not have to read. I see the word, and then I hear the teacher say, "Dan on the rug. Ok, Dillan, point to Dan." Easy, intentional pointing I think; then I hand her the book. She is not surprised. Her attitude is that I can't understand the instruction, and so I got it wrong. I listened to her say, "point," but handed her the book instead, not intending to. I lose myself once I give the book to her because I can't prove anything anyway. I go into behaviors that the teacher misunderstands. I am not having behaviors to get out of work. I am having all other kinds of thoughts and feelings. I have heard with my ears what the teacher said and understand with my mind the directions (having read the word "Dan" as soon as I saw it), but then making my hand stop and point is another action that I never have been able to do. Then I go crazy thinking about all of this and can't stay still. I can't really point to anything so what is it they have in their minds that they are teaching me anyway? The teachers only testing measurements are to try to work our minds with questions that need movement to respond, but without the mind in full control of the body, a student would never pass the test. It is hard to sit any longer, so I move and try to leave.

I move around the room, not ever learning how to communicate, only that I am trapped and forced to comply in a world of easy lessons that I cannot prove I already know. I can read the easy words, and even know the complicated ones that people say won't make sense to me. In desperation, I listen to people, to their demands, only because if I don't then it will be really bad. They will tell me to stop, then warn me, then take the toys I love, then have me try again and again. I decide not to experience that if I can avoid it. Many days anxiety takes over. Each time I attempt to stop a behavior, it gets worse. As I am spinning out of control in the grip of my anxiety, it's not easy to deal with the simple and disappointed talk I hear from others in my direction. I can see on their faces that they are disgusted or frustrated with my actions. They are not looking at a boy, but a hollow shell that will never be full of anything but autism. I am eating crayons instead of coloring the outline of a hand that I am supposed to. Then I would be laughing and acting like everything is funny, when I am crying inside. The desks have so much dirt on them, so I spit on certain marks and rub them to see movement that I can control.

Unheard minds, again and again, lose so much hope since we are expected to amount to little more than silly trials meant to help handle our autistic behaviors, instead of first believing in us more. The prison of my mind did not hold my voice trapped forever though. It was a long search for an educator who could help me unlock the cage. Obviously, because you are reading my own free words now, my search came to a victory as I found someone who held a new perspective. That search was long and hard, however.

A New Perspective Brings Hope

"I learned that I could spell not only one simple word, but entire thoughts that had always been locked away so deep only I knew they had ever existed."

Every day I dreamed of finding an experience that my special education teachers would never bring to the classrooms for people like me. To not have the help I needed to be heard was like being trapped in the worst place imaginable. It would have been easier to get through if I were the kind of student that teachers and people believed in. Each person is wired differently, but my autistic wiring crossed my body signals so badly that teachers never saw anything they could believe in. Their way to my education was to have control of my behavior. My autism took over easily because much of my mind was finding its own information to learn. I admit I was extremely broken in soul and spirit.

Dealing with their academics was like a stationary bike, always peddling and going nowhere—easy lessons repeating day after day in place of a real school education. Much of my mind wanted to know about the world like any other student, but it always was impossible. What my teachers believed about me influenced what they taught me. And these teaching practices were the problem, not my autism.

Finally, I met a teacher who had the courage to look these assumptions in the face and started me on the amazing journey of learning to control not only my body, but also my mind, so I could spell the thoughts I always had.

One letter at a time, I got to spell a thought that had never existed aloud before. The day I started spelling out even single words was like being freed. I learned that I could spell not only one simple word, but entire thoughts that had always been locked away so deep only I knew they had ever existed. I could show that I totally understood everything.

My new teacher felt that I basically was totally controlled by my autism. Like answering my prayers, she got it right. I had no control, but when I spelled words with her kind of tough, insisting ways, it challenged my autistic head. She taught, had faith in me, and always believed that real communication can happen if the teacher can look through the autism toward the mind underneath. A teacher should have faith, and teach what we need even when we are at our worst.

My time with this brilliant teacher who finally reached toward the core of my voice and unlocked typing with her methods was sadly short. I had to go back home. Back home meant the schools where this new oasis of typing would be a long way away. I dreaded this return to the silence, but I was saved from an eternal fate of simple classes and simple ideas. It turned out that my typing teacher was not the only open mind in the world, and I soon met another.

Finally Learning

"Nothing makes me more hopeful than knowing people believe in me."

Over the years in school, I really had gotten used to the idea that I quite possibly might never be able to show any of my teachers that I learned ongoing all the time. I not only knew so much already, I was learning new things too, all without being intentionally taught. I learned back in my earliest days by listening, and later got to read the words no one thought I could. In class, I was given really simple work. Only by chance would I find more interesting words in books and in notes on teachers' desks. On the long road to finding an education that is appropriate for an autistic student, I am the first to say that I understand why schools are set up the way they are. Students' knowledge must be proved, but how can it be when autism is looked at as a cognitive disability? I had no way to prove what I knew or was learning. The school that I went to had no way to teach me this new method of communication. The teachers cared, but were in a completely different view of instruction for students like me. Poor hand control and body control left me at the point of despair.

That all changed the day I heard my mom on the phone talking to someone I was going to have as my new support person in school. Ongoing therapy over the years left me feeling hopeless and frustrated, so at first I heard nothing but doubts in my mind, but then I met her. Deb was open to having a different way of working with me, and learning to support me to spell out my thoughts letter by letter. She was the one person who would train her own mind and learn to support a method of communication that would take me out of those autism classes and into a whole new world.

The days I started in general education unfortunately came late in middle school. I stayed in the autism class until my new school support, Deb, could see a way to get me out. The school allowed Deb and me to take time away from the autism classroom to begin building my skills so that I could have reliable communication and take a real test. I had to learn so much about controlling certain things about myself. A lot of fear and anxiety had me crippled. Getting a handle on my fears, when I was allowed to try to start having some classes in general education, was as important as communicating what I understood.

In a way, I had more to learn than any other 7th grader. I missed the learning others had in their earlier education. I had minimal practice with sitting and listening to a lecture. The classes gave me so much more than a better curriculum. My teachers tried to have an open mind about me and get to learn about autism too. Making the teachers nervous easily is the first trial to get over. We do not belong in their idea of a perfect classroom. They do not say it, but it is plain to see. I need a typical education, but really not in a typical way. I will move, I will make noise, and sometimes I need to leave class. But to leave class is different than to be blocked from class by people who do not believe I ever really belonged there. In classes with people not familiar with autism that is so visible, it can be hard to make a good impression. I am more work for a teacher who has so much to contend with before they let autism into the room. It is only possible to overcome this all with a team behind me to keep my autism in needed peace, so the teacher can forget it is there and teach things I want to know.

My autism is full of erratic needs and constant impulses, and is tough to handle without the right support. I am not always able to stay rational, so it is critical for someone near me to keep me from drowning in autism. It is not so bad when things do go crazy. It happens and then it passes, and it is a poor reason to keep us locked away in a small class of boredom and repeated lessons of washing hands and days of the week.

During my middle school years, I moved on to spending more and more time in general education. The classes were so incredible. I heard so many new and interesting things. Those days were sort of scary too. I never knew when I might lose control, and when my last ounce of strength to stay in my seat would wear out. Then I had the inhospitable experience of a few teachers with fear of my behaviors. That may have stopped me in my tracks, but I had Deb there in every second of those moments when I felt uncertain. She believed in me, got through my fear, and helped me to have confidence in my communication. Once I could have the protection of a really strong and determined support person, I could handle anything. Ideas that I never dreamed could happen did. I got to take real classes. I had a person who understood in many ways about autism and had learned to read my words as I typed, and saw me, totally, for the first time in my life. Only with a person by your side who has total faith and confidence in your having thoughts that are intelligent even when you are out of control will you ever have any hope to be able to handle all of the challenges that really never stop coming.

One of my teachers had the best handle on ways of teaching. He really made learning a fun experience for all his students. In his class, we learned about how GMO food can be harmful and be beneficial depending on how you looked at it. I had never been able to have that kind of learning experience before. I had other teachers teach me to repeat information but never to have an investigative mind and to share my opinions too. I loved that!

I headed into 8th grade going into more general education classes than I could imagine was ever possible. I could give answers to questions and share them with my classmates to amaze them that this totally awkward and sometimes-strange guy is as smart as they are.

Having had the opportunity to be a student in regular classes was so incredibly liberating, however, I saw my old friends still in those autism classes going through their days like I used to. I had gotten so far in my own life that I decided I had to try to speak out and make the life I lead a possibility for all others like me too.

Making My Message Heard

> "I had to become a communicator to advocate for myself, and I do it every time I type because then you see me."

Early on in middle school I gained opportunities that almost no other student like me has had before. The opportunity to point to a letter board or type on a keyboard was the start of an amazing, out-of-this-world experience. Several teachers already accepted me as a smart student, capable like anyone else to achieve and contribute my own thoughts in class. I mostly can remember feeling so happy that I was finally being seen and heard. Then came an opportunity one day that certainly felt inspiring and depressing all at once. In 8th grade, some students are chosen to give a speech at graduation. Anyone could try; all they had to do was submit a speech. I thought maybe I should do it, but was insecure to say the least. I felt hidden before, and I really wanted to be seen and heard, but each time I imagined going in front of all the people at my graduation, I became afraid that it might be too much, and I would lose control. That's the depressing part—that I wanted to speak but was scared to try. So, I asked the people who loved and knew me best, and to my surprise they all said, "Yes!" I had so many doubts, but only one certainty: I had my support person by my side. Deb understood all of my fears, and helped me to feel confident in myself in a way I had never been able to experience before. Her confidence in my ability to handle the stress naturally gave me the courage to take a chance. Outside of classes, I spent every minute typing my speech. The entire process took me weeks. I had only one choice that I knew I should make, and so I entered my speech into the contest and waited. Then it happened.… I was chosen to speak at my graduation. It was unbelievable and totally frightening and exciting all at once.

It was a beautiful Southern California day. There were so many people, but all I could do to manage all the looks and stares was to focus on their minds and what they might be thinking. Then I had a realization, and a notion began to grow and take form in my mind. Maybe I could actually change people's perceptions that autistic students like me would never be able to give a speech or even think the thoughts that I wrote.

Early decisions can place you on a road you never knew existed. In my case, I lived in the most incredible time in my life that day. I remember I was nervous, and each one of the other speakers was too. The only thing that gave me the confidence in myself was the decision that I had to try to share my thoughts with as many listeners that cared to try to have an open mind to this strange kid. I hoped that maybe some or at least half of the crowd might get it—that we are smart and capable.

A local news crew was there that day, and in a few minutes, many more heard and allowed the intense debate to take hold in their minds. I put out a message to thousands of people that spelled words can give insight into an autistic person's mind, and that what appears on the outside is not necessarily who you are meeting.

This moment happened at a major transition for me. I went on from that point to high school, but the moment you start high school there is a looming question that hounds your every step. Each teacher reminded me every day that this was nothing more than preparation for what comes next. I had fought so hard to become a fully included student in middle school and high school that the thought had never even occurred to me that there would be more after achieving this goal. Where would I go? What would I do? I had to decide what my hard fought education was amounting to.

Where I Go Next

Seeing into the distant future is not a power I have in my host of mental abilities. The future is filled with hopes which build a picture of shifting fantasies and sometimes fears.

I would love to imagine a house and a fast car and my arm around a pretty, loving wife. I would imagine all the simple things a person would want for himself.

There are a million layers to my goals that I must contend with. I dream of making eggs in a home alone. I imagine getting dressed and going to the living room without getting caught in the meticulous task of lining plastic animals across my bed for hours. I imagine taking a long shower because I feel like it, and no one crashes through the thin wall of my privacy to make sure I haven't become stuck compulsively picking my teeth for all time, until I am saved by their intrusion.

I imagine so many tiny indulgences you enjoy without even knowing it. Even the most basic one might be unattainable after a lifetime of working on it. The ones I can achieve are at least as distant to me as the house and car and wife are to my peers. I am not sad for it, and I do not want you to be. I only want you to see what a big question it is to ask where I want to be in my future years.

My goal is to be a normal, independent man, but I do have to temper that goal with the reality of my autism. I will have a college degree and I will advocate for my community of silent students looking for a voice. I am certain I will have a way to live with greater independence. I may or may not have achieved any of the million layers of my fantasy life, but the one thing I can say for certain is that I will be fighting and striving to make them all happen.

The Others Like Me

Attitudes about this misunderstood and often hard to explain condition have placed many autistic people in a hidden world sometimes never to be heard from. We have been defined in terms that come from decades-old behavioral thoughts and theories. Through the door of communication, some of us autistics have now been freed from the astounding and almost immovable perceptions that have clouded people's views of us.

For myself, there is a momentous effort to gain a valued education involving many people fighting to make it possible. When I think of what I want for others, it falls on having fewer obstacles like the ones that I have faced. I would like to see other spellers and typers supported instead of battled. I would rather see the system of effort work toward propelling forward the outmoded methods of trying to teach students with autism. It would be great to see a school where the only thing to struggle against is our autism.

I long to see more of us in classes that have no distinctions. Being in so many classes felt lonely as the only one who typed. Spelled or typed communication should be an option first to autistic nonspeaking students. Every student needs their right to communication respected, and that includes each student being supported in the mode of communication that draws out their most genuine expression.

The Guide to Reaching Your Students

> *"What I needed were my teachers to be my instruments. I needed them to learn and realize that autism is not a list of behaviors, it's an identity with human complexity and like any other it deserves to be viewed with respect. If they could have realized that, I would have played the most powerful music with them as my instruments of learning. Our voice is hidden from the world of educators. All they think, they learned from minds that are not autistic. All they learned could never have helped them to help me."*

Suggestions I can give educators to support students' learning and communicating starts with believing that they are capable of understanding, thinking about, and processing the knowledge of the world around them. No progress will ever be made in a classroom where each adult sees only empty heads and broken minds in their students. If you are teaching 20-year-olds the alphabet and days of the week, then stop it! They have heard it for 20 years. They know it. They might have challenges telling you the day, but they know it, and it is a terribly lazy waste to explain it every morning like you are doing something.

Talk about something new like the origins of the Julian calendar, or something interesting that happened 100 years ago today. Then you can start to explore some new ways for your students to express and communicate these new ideas. Take it to heart that each student is a thinking person.

The people in charge of making policy in education often believe they already have all the answers, and their rigid thinking makes it difficult for them to accept that they may be wrong or have incomplete information. A person must be willing to question themselves and the entire weight of a system of education built around false premises that students like me are hopelessly simple-minded. That is not only difficult to do, but dangerous to your career because the education system is rigid and hostile to rogue elements that seek to do things differently. But if you are starting with the belief that your students are mentally competent, then you will see that you have no choice as a compassionate being but to move forward to build communication and learning in a meaningful way, because doing less is cruelty.

Go on and think about all the things you have been taught in the education you were given, and then take it out of your mind, and push the limits on your perceptions of autism beyond what it is that you see, and look at all of us in another mindset. In reaching out to autistic students, educators can do the following:

Believing in a Student Like Me
Looks Like This

Talk to me when I get to class even if there is no time to wait for a response; usually a hello does not need a big reply. In class discussion, ask for my thoughts and do not accept my outward appearance of not listening as a sign of my level of interest. Ask me, move on to give me time to type my reply, but then come back to me and I can share. Access to education in a classroom depends on you providing me with a chance at all curriculum and expecting a lot from me; but be flexible and ready to accept that my best is about quality, not simply completing the task for a sign of my understanding of a concept.

Supporting My Motor Needs

I am autistic and ready to learn, but not in the traditional sense. People expect so little of us and they have been taught that we are not capable of long, complicated thinking. They have ideas of how to teach us, which include hand-over-hand practice to make choices, but then they drive the hands to the choices of their design and there is no chance for my mind to insist on a choice that I intend. They then ask us questions that rely on motor control, such as pointing to an answer, to prove our knowledge. They do not realize that I do not have the intentional control to get my hand where I wanted it to go. Their early attempts to have my hand move to the right object (i.e., hand over hand) does not train the motor area of the brain, and until they reach that piece of the mind, they leave me without a way to make choices with earnest intent. They've got to stop that type of teaching—it's not early education, it's early torture! In school, I needed a teacher more believing in my mind, not in my hands' abilities.

I know that some doubter is reading here now and I know the argument that rises up in their mind. If I cannot control myself to point to simple cards, how do I control my hands to point to strings of countless letters to produce thoughts? It is a matter of practice first, but also of motivation. There is no reward in pointing to "blue" that ever mattered. A piece of candy, a toy, a smile and praise—all of these never mattered when the task was so stupid to me. I was on a treadmill going nowhere. With typing, my motives were freedom. I put so much work and focus into typing that I could finally overcome the hardship of my poor motor system to make my thoughts known. Engaging in dialogue mattered to me, pointing to "blue" never could when it meant my teacher would just consider my education complete because I had accomplished the mindless nothing of her command. I have fought for years to gain the precision of my typing hand, and even still, can be a struggle to make my thoughts heard. There are many words on this page, but you do not know the time and work it took to make them appear.

Providing Meaningful and Effective Support

Never had I imagined that one day there would have been an individual who used determination and belief in a way that unsuccessful teaching approaches could not have attained. The kind of educational approach I needed was an intense combination of working the mind and body in order to get to know each thought.

Having technical skills in supporting a typer's communication is only one piece to the puzzle of autism. I needed a multidisciplinary approach. I practiced for months with varied strategies of support to spell and type answers to academic problems, and to say what I thought and control my uncooperative body. Some days I was able to handle more on my own, but I needed someone to believe in my ability to gain independence while still recognizing when I needed additional support.

Not only is the strategy or intervention important, it's also knowing when to use it and when not to. A strategy may be helpful in one class, and dangerous in another. Gaining regulation is first. Then I am able to get to a place where my rational mind is in control and I feel somewhat calm and able to succeed. It is important to have a support person who is flexible and ready to help me acquire the ability to navigate and perform what I need to be a student in a classroom.

Most importantly, I have to talk about the emotional piece to my educational experience. If I had a support partner that only focused on typing and academics, it wouldn't be enough because I would not be a real person to them. In taking my feelings and experiences into account, I become whole in my support person's mind and then I know I'm not alone in this world. I need to be heard. I am not heard when therapists are using some strategy alone and not really talking to me.

Relating vs. Controlling

An uncooperative body is the most difficult part of needing help. People have always thought that I would intentionally act in this way— that it was a decision I made. I now understand that an overwhelming amount of my behavior could be going against therapists' actions to always control my autism and not relate to it.

To relate to my autism is to try to see it as part of who I am, and to lose preconceptions that we are not whole in mind. I found that when my autism was the focus in a therapist's design to help me, I was never even a thought in their mind. We lead lives in isolation, and to type opens doors to personal relating, which is the real meaning of communication.

What to Do When the Autistic Head Wakes Up

I see why it is difficult to know our minds are sharp, and I have moments where nothing seems like it will ever get through my wall of autism. Those times I am crazy laughing and throwing things and "being bad," as you would say if you are thinking of me as a simple child. I see frustration from others when I am like that because, yes, I am frustrating. But you cannot win over my autism from a place of anger. You cannot control me. It is that simple. But it's not because I am too strong, or better, or right, it is because I'm a teenager who just causes trouble sometimes. So stick with me and be calm. Try in new ways to reach me. Have the patience to maybe just wait until the storm passes, but do not make strong demands for changes in an instant because it won't happen and you will just get mad. I need to be in a place of self-control and it is hard to get there from the path of "just ignore it, he can't help himself." I see the need for balance where I can take responsibility, but people have to understand that my moments of trouble just look different, and they must measure their reactions.

Let Us Lead the Charge

The kind of practices and policies that are in place for students like me are all supposed to be helpful in providing us with an education that is full of challenge, but all those policies and practices come from the ideas that autistic people are not to be overwhelmed or challenged, because you might have to see our behavior. Now my behavior is why I am not believed in, but I would never give in to your ideas of what is supposed to be the appearance of appropriate behavior. Noises and movement are who I am. Accept it or not, but do not avoid challenging me or deny me a real education.

Reading my story is not enough—it is a beginning. Take what I have said with you as you look to other people who are impacted by autism. Take lessons from each typer in this book and really believe that every autistic child can achieve this level of expression if you reach out with an open mind.

SECTION 3

*Triumphs and Obstacles
in Navigating
the Educational Maze*

7

Expectations

Henry Frost

Henry Frost is an 20-year-old autistic high school student and nationally acclaimed advocate for inclusion. Henry is a blogger for Ollibean and was recently a guest lecturer at Princeton University. In 2012, Henry faced disability-based discrimination when he was denied entry to the middle school across the street from his home in Tampa, FL. Henry started the "I STAND WITH HENRY" campaign to take action against disability-based segregation. Henry's social media campaign garnered widespread international support. In 2013, Henry received the Autistic Self Advocacy Network's Award. Henry has presented at conferences around the country, provided in-depth interviews for National Public Radio, State Impact, The Orlando Sentinel, Huffington Post, *and been quoted in numerous publications. Henry's writing is included in the book* Typed Words Loud Voices *as well as* Halo's Voices. *Most importantly, he has empowered others who have faced discrimination to demand change and an equal education in their community. Henry can be found at @istandwithhenry on Facebook and Twitter.*

Communication Is Always Happening

Every person communicates but not every person has people that listen. My parents listened. I have always communicated but not in a way most understand. My family understood but most of the world did not. Before I learned to communicate by typing I communicated in many ways. My mom says since I was a small baby my eyes have always

115

communicated so much. I have multiple disabilities; I am autistic, profoundly deaf in my left ear and hard of hearing in my right and I have physical disabilities. It was easy to see that movement and motor planning were hard for me. And my family assumed that my movement differences were the reasons I did not talk, they did not assume my lack of speech was lack of understanding or motivation.

Growing up, my parents told me I made it easy to see how many thoughts I had and it was their job to help me find a way to express them. They found the right people to teach me to communicate in a language the world understands. I am considered lucky because I did not grow up believing the problem was me. No kid should ever grow up feeling that they or their neurology are the problems.

My house was full of language. There were captions on TV and words all over my house. My parents read children's books and homemade books full of the pictures and vocabulary of our life. These language tools from my Deaf and Hard of Hearing teacher and mom helped me learn to read by three. It would help all autistic kids to be taught this way.

I went to an inclusive preschool when I was three and met Stephanie, my speech therapist and friend. Today, fifteen years later, she is my friend. Stephanie gave me what every nonspeaking kid needs— respect and the foundation for my preferred way to communicate with the world. Stephanie gave me a piece of paper that I could always have with me. This piece of paper had the combinations to every English word, it was a laminated QWERTY keyboard. Predictable, beautiful letters in the exact same order as our computer keyboard at home.

Stephanie explained to me that I could spell the words I loved by pointing to each letter in their order. When we learned the name of the color blue at school, other kids moved their mouths and "blue" came out. Stephanie pointed to B-L-U-E, then she showed me how to point to B-L-U-E. Stephanie showed me the power of spelling.

The other kids loved their teddy bears and blankets, I loved my keyboard. I carried it everywhere with me. I still do.

When I was four Stephanie told my mom about Soma and the Rapid Prompting Method. When Soma came to a workshop in Tampa and I got to work with her for the first time; I wish all my teachers were like Soma. My mom and my Stephanie started teaching me academics using RPM. When I was in kindergarten, I learned what other kids in kindergarten learned. When I was in first grade, same thing, and on and on. RPM gave me a way to participate.

Sometimes I used basic sign language and my own signs to communicate what I needed. I made my own signs for my favorite things. The sign for Keyboard—two hands in the air above my shoulders. It looks like the two hands praise emoji. And "Chevy"—first two fingers of right hand tap the palm of left hand. I also used signs to communicate in the conversations that happen every day, like saying "Good morning" or "Good night."

But it would be seven long years before I used a keyboard for more than academics or facts about people and places. That is almost 2,500 days before I typed about my hopes or my dreams. Eighty-four months before I gave real input into decisions about my life. No person should have to wait so long to use their voice for their life. People think I am lucky because I was taught to use a keyboard, taught to read and taught age appropriate academics. No person would think a neurotypical person was lucky for those same reasons. But, I only had a trained communication partner for two and a half months my entire time in public school: in fifth grade for a month and a half and maybe a month total in middle school. It would have been a different experience for me with a communication partner.

Communication and education are human rights. No more waiting for rights that are already ours. All people should have access to communication, be taught literacy skills and have curriculum that is age appropriate.

An Attempt at Inclusion

My home life was full of words, belief, respect and accommodations. But I did not have this same life in other places. This was hard. I did not understand why I was treated differently than other people. I did not understand why communicating what I knew was easier for me at home than at school. My parents did not use any labels or even tell me I had a disability. They just talked about how something like my hearing aid helped amplify sounds that were hard for me to hear without it. My family made a mistake not talking to me about autism and disability.

I have talked to my mom about this mistake and she apologized. She told me that before I was born, she and my dad did not have much experience with children with disabilities. Their first introduction was with Early Intervention; where specialists pointed out and labeled what was not "typical," and then prescribed hours and hours of therapy to fix it. She said it was this weird alternate universe, that she and my dad did not think of me as a list of deficits. My mom said the best early intervention for them as parents would have been meeting and learning from disabled people.

My sisters were four and two when I was born. We are close in age and feeling. I always loved being with them, I still do. When I was 5, I was excited to go to kindergarten at the same school where they went. I thought I would be with my neighbors too. But I was not allowed to do what my sisters did. I could not join my friends in the kindergarten class. I would only be allowed in a segregated class at their school. My parents decided to send me to a school in another neighborhood. This school had an inclusive kindergarten class and an autism class. I went to both.

The inclusion was only for kindergarten at this school. My mom knew I deserved the same opportunities and education that my sisters had. I would not get the same opportunities in a segregated class. So, my mom and her friend started Bird Academy, an elementary school for students with learning disabilities to be taught the general education curriculum.

It was the only way I could get access to the general education curriculum. I went to school there from kindergarten to 5th grade. And it was okay. For a while.

When I went to Bird Academy I had two lives, one at home and one at school. At home, everyone knew I could learn and had high expectations. When I did academics at home, everyone made sure there was not a lot of background noise and they sat on my right side so I could hear. They found what I needed to learn and participate, and they did it. It was not a big deal because I was not the only person who needed accommodations, everyone in my family did. Two people need written lists to remember things, one person needed glasses, one needed more time for chores, one needed alarm reminders, one needed to exercise before learning, two needed limited distractions, and three needed time alone after a big day. It was just part of our life.

My family knew I was smart and could learn. But at school, most of the teachers did not. There were two teachers that treated me like a real student. Maybe these teachers treated me differently because they knew me outside school. They saw me communicating and learning at my house so they knew I could do the same at school. They saw that in my house, the TV had closed captions, I had an overlay that made my computer a touchscreen and other accommodations. These teachers made sure I had them at school, too. I learned so much from them. If teachers treat their students as learners, their students will learn.

I was seven years old when I was in Miss R's class. Miss R was one of those teachers who knew me outside of school and saw me as a learner. Even though I did not have a communication partner, Miss R made sure I had the same accommodations at school that I did at home. I was seven when I was in her class. She let me take tests in a quiet room. She let me point to the multiple-choice questions instead of circling them. She let me type the answers to the spelling tests instead of using a pencil. Miss R also let me be the line leader and be part of my second-grade class. I was happy, I learned a lot and I made good grades.

One day Miss R was taking my class to the playground. I was happy because we just got our spelling tests back and I made an A. We walked out the door to the playground and the school speech therapist came around the corner. Miss R told her about my spelling grade. The speech therapist said that was impossible, there was no way I could spell those words. She said all of this in front of everyone. She told me to go with her to get my test out of my desk. Then she took me into her office and said I had to take the test again.

The speech therapist was right, I could not spell any of the words in her office. My knowledge did not change. I knew how to spell those words but my anxiety and fear would not let me show it. My body would not listen to my brain.

I thought something was wrong with me. Now I know teachers' attitudes affect performance. Experiments like the Brown-Eyed Blue-Eyed discrimination experiment by Jane Elliot and other experiments about people's attitudes show what I experienced with the speech therapist. The problem with my performance was not me.

Accommodations and Attitudes

It is time to clear up the misunderstanding about autism and the problem with generalized or carry over skills. The problem is not with the autistic student's skill being carried over to different environments. One problem is that the necessary accommodations are not being carried over to different environments. Accommodations are not optional for access. Another potential problem is the attitude of the skill tester. The tester believes the person will not do well and they don't.

Bird Academy was not accessible like my home. The challenges were access and attitudes, not academics. It was hard to hear the teacher because of all the noise. And, I could only communicate with one teacher. Going to a school all day where people think you are incapable wears away your confidence. President Bush talks about "the soft bigotry of low expectations," I can tell you there is nothing soft about the bigotry of low expectations.

The ways the people have revealed their prejudice helped me learn to recognize ableist behavior. Bigotry has a predictable pattern. Sorting ableists into groups is helpful to me because I do not have to think about what is happening. I see their prejudice is not about me. As you will see in the behaviors of two common groups: Angry Ableist (Angry Abe) and Entertaining Ableist (The Standup).

The Angry Ableist does not hide their bigotry. Angry Abe never talks directly to you, they talk about you. Abe did "not sign up to teach a student like you" so they do not teach you. Abe does not believe that you can learn so he does not waste his time. The Angry Ableist wants you to feel their disdain so you will leave their classroom.

Entertaining Ableist seems harmless at first. Do not be fooled. Entertaining Ableist loves to make their "special kids" happy but they do not think you can learn. The Standup will sing songs, act out preschool videos, make funny noises, or script with you. Proceed with caution when interacting with the Standup. Engaging the Entertaining Ableist the first time they try out their routine with you will only encourage them. The Standup will feel so good about giving a disabled person such joy. The Standup will think you have a special connection and they are the "autistic whisperer." The Standup will repeat the same routine the next time they see you. If you do not laugh they will repeat it again. And again. If you still have not laughed, The Standup will look at you with worry on their face. Then, they will look at the aide or teacher or parent with you and tell them you must be having a hard day.

Then you will stand there while they talk about adding joke time to your social skills group. The next time The Standup sees you they will try their routine again, but this time you will laugh because you know that is what they want. The Standup will feel good and connected to you again. This same routine can go on for years. Then one day your love of predictability takes over and you start the script instead of The Standup starting it. You are now stuck doing something you do not want to do, but you must do. The Standup will not remember their part in starting the routine and their incorrect ideas about inflexible and obsessive interests of autistic people will be reinforced.

For now, I won't elaborate on the characteristics of the other types of ableism I most commonly encounter, which I designate as Ableist Grandma, Savior Ableist (Mission Possible), Eager Ableist (High Five Buddy), and the Special Gifts Ableist (Touched by an Angel). I hope that the portraits of Angry Abe and The Standup demonstrate how attempts to communicate with autistic people will backfire if both parties aren't capable of engaging with mutual respect.

Segregated Education

When I started at Bird Academy we were not segregated by perceived levels of ability. By the time I was in third grade, my school for students with learning disabilities added a new self-contained-special education-segregated class for students at the bottom of the disability hierarchy.

Placement in the disability hierarchy is based on how you communicate. Clear verbal speech is on top, hard to understand verbal speech is in the middle and no verbal speech is at the bottom. Your placement in the hierarchy usually determines your access to education and community. This disability hierarchy exists everywhere: in society, classrooms, hospitals, work, and in families. It is even in the disability community. Every day, false assumptions about intelligence and communication deny life opportunities.

Inclusion is not just allowing students that use a wheelchair or have ADD or dyslexia in class. Inclusion is including all learners. Those schools include students at the top of the hierarchy and segregate the students they place at the bottom of the hierarchy. The earlier you are segregated, the smaller your life opportunities. Everyone deserves a life of opportunity.

The staff used the disability hierarchy to choose which students needed to be separated from the other students in my school. Because I do not communicate like the majority, I was one of students they chose to separate from the rest of the school.

The segregated class was different than the other classes at Bird Academy. It had students of all ages, from 6 to 12 years old. The students in the class were as alike and different as any students in the school. Except for one thing. Speech. Our speech was not like the others.

I was the only person that did not use my mouth to speak. But some did not speak much, some speech was hard to understand, and some speech just sounded different. Many educators do not understand that ability to learn does not correlate with articulation ability or reliable speech.

Those of us in the segregated class were not around our old friends from second grade anymore. Everything was separate. The classroom was separated from all the other classes. It was located on the side of the building with the school's daycare. Our lunch time was separate, our recess was separate. We were Separate. We were Other.

There were no spelling tests to retake with the speech therapist, because we did not have tests. We were too busy with the weather and the days of the week. Every day we worked on this. Over and over. And Over. And every day after school, I went to another school to be tutored in academics. And when I was finished, I went home and did more academics.

Fourth and Fifth grade were exactly the same. Same classroom. Same students. Same teacher. Same handouts, calendar and weather. It was a slow torture.

At home, I pointed to a letter board for academics but I did not do this for my feelings. I did not know how to tell my mom and Russ that I hated this class. I would wake up in the middle of the night and hide my uniform. When they asked why I did not want to go to school I could not explain it.

We had a meeting to talk with the principal about why I did not want to go to school anymore. The principal had noticed I was not interested in school. She thought I was depressed and maybe anesthesia from my foot surgery caused it.

I was depressed, but not from anesthesia. I was depressed because segregation is depressing. It is depressing being separated from everyone else at school. It was depressing being taught the same thing for three years. I was ten years old and depressed. I needed to find a way out.

A Message to Parents

Another lesson from my parents' mistakes: do not allow your elementary school student to be put in a segregated class. First, all supports and services must be exhausted before a change of placement is considered.

My parents did not know at that time what placement in a segregated class meant. When the principal suggested the new class for me, my mom did not know it was a one-way ticket.

My parents heard: "This class will be better for Henry. There is a better student-teacher ratio. There is more speech therapy. Henry will not have the stress of testing." The reality of a self-contained, segregated special education class is:

1. Your old friends do not want to hang out with you.
2. You are subjected to a different curriculum than general education curriculum.
3. You typically do not get the opportunity to earn a regular high school diploma.
4. There are many ages in one class.
5. Life skills are a priority over academics.
6. Writing your name with a pencil is a priority over typing it on a keyboard.

7. Your re-entry into the general education class depends on taking a test.

8. The questions on this test are from the general curriculum. It is hard to know the information you are not taught.

I still had my tutor and my mom teaching me after school. I did not like going to school after school but it was the only chance to learn. My tutor and my mom taught me the general education curriculum at home. Proving I could re-enter the general education classroom would be harder if I did not go to school after school for all those years.

Autistic Freedom

When I was 11, I saw the film *Wretches and Jabberers*. My family's company, Ollibean, had two screenings in our town. Tracy Thresher and Larry Bissonette, the stars of the documentary, came to my house for dinner the night before the screening at the Tampa Museum of Art. It was the first time I was around people that type to communicate. I was with my people. My sisters, mom, Russ, Nai Nai (my grandmother) Leigh my aunt, Tracy, Larry, Harvey and Pascal sat around my dining room table and talked about communication, inclusion and civil rights. We typed and talked until midnight. It was one of the best nights of my life.

The next day Tracy, Larry, Harvey and Pascal came for lunch at our house. Stephanie, my speech therapist came too. It was more conversation that I will never forget. That night we went to the Museum for the screening of *Wretches and Jabberers*. All the people in the audience loved the movie like I did. After Tracy and Larry did a Q & A. The next day we were together all day for lunch and the screening at Tampa Theatre and another long dinner of typing and talking.

For the first time in my life I felt part of the world outside my home. I felt connected to Tracy and Larry. I did not want them to leave.

My family saw this and made it possible for me to be around them. I went to a Communication and Inclusion Conference at MIT Media Lab and met more typers and found more acceptance.

We drove from Boston to Vermont to visit Tracy and Larry. And my aunt Leigh and cousins met us there. The first day we went on a ferry on Lake Champlain with Pascal, Tracy and Jeanette. My family, Tracy, Larry, Harvey, and Larry's sister had dinner at Pascal's. At these dinners, people give you time to type your answers. People do not talk all at one time. I could be part of the conversation. Talkers do not know the feeling of not being part of life's moments.

The next day we went to Larry's studio and he talked to us about his art. We also went to Tracy's office for more typing. That is when I joined the World Intelligence Tour.

I found a different world. Everything changed. I started typing about more than academics. I typed everything and the world opened. I met autistic people. I met so many people who wanted my opinion about life. People outside of my family who knew I had thoughts and ideas. People that did not need to test me before treating me with respect.

I could flap. I could stim. I could be myself. Everyone could. People wanted to talk to me. Being accepted by people outside my family changed my life. For the first time, I felt part of something, I knew I was not alone. I felt the chance for a life that I choose.

My parents and I knew I could not go back to the segregated class at Bird Academy. Now we knew I had the right to accommodations to access the curriculum. My new class had to be accessible and I needed my iPad to communicate. I am deaf in my left ear and hard of hearing in my right ear. To hear a teacher in a classroom I need an FM system. An FM system is a microphone and a receiver. The teacher wears the microphone and her voice goes right in my ear.

The educators at Bird Academy liked us when my mom and her friends got the charter and raised money for their playgrounds. They liked us until she advocated for my rights. When mom and Russ told them I needed an FM system that worked with my hearing aid, Mrs. John, the head of the school, did not like that. Mrs. John said the charter school's charter was not for deaf and hard of hearing students, so they did not need to provide access. Mrs. John said maybe Bird Academy was not the right school for me.

My disabilities did not change from 2004 to 2011, something else changed. Knowing my access and educational rights changed. A disability rights group went with us to the Individualized Education Program (IEP) meeting and helped me get out of the segregated class and back into the general education class.

The door to general education class was now open for me but the attitudes about me as a class member were still closed. The school and the teachers did not want me to stay in that class. For the first time in five years I was not welcome at Bird Academy. Feeling their anger was worse than being bored in the segregated class. I felt their resentment. My thoughts and my body got more disconnected under their anger. The more they believed I did not belong the harder it got. I got in trouble for the first time at school. Then, I started getting in trouble every day.

We made videos of me working on academics at home to show the teachers. We made videos showing how I used text on Proloquo2go, a communication app on the iPad. Because I did not have a communication partner at school, I had to use preprogrammed text. We thought when they saw these videos it would help change their attitude. But, they did not change their attitude or expectations. It is for people to change because they must admit there were many students they underestimated. I believe this is changing as science proves the old attitudes limiting learning are obsolete.

The school told my parents that the academic stress was causing behavior problems. They said taking the standardized tests would make it worse and it was best to go back to the alternative assessment.

Learning to Self-Advocate

We worked on a plan to make it through my fifth-grade year at Bird School and then change to the middle school across the street from my house. My parents hired a communication specialist to support me at school. This was the first and only time in my life I had a full time communication partner at school. We talked to many people about how to prepare for this. I talked to my mentor and other autistic people. My mom talked to inclusion specialists, typers and parents of typers that were in the general education class.

That spring, my school experiences became unbearable and we decided I would leave Bird Academy to be homeschooled for the rest of the year. Then I tried to enroll for 6th grade at Blank Middle School across the street from my house. The school said I could not attend because of my disability. I could not believe it.

That summer I decided to stand up for myself and all neurodiverse students. I got advice from my mentors, Tracy Thresher and Ari Ne'eman. I would not accept segregation anymore.

I worked on advocating to gain entry and preparing for that entry all summer. I continued working through my neighbor's 5th grade classwork to be ready for 6th grade. On August 23, the lesson was on Dr. Martin Luther King and Cesar Chavez. Reading more of Dr. Martin Luther King's work on what would have been my dad's 45th birthday, everything became clear.

I typed "Today I read about Martin Luther King. The Civil Rights Act of 1964 granted equal rights to all people. I am a person. I want these rights. I want to go to school in my neighborhood. Why can't I?"

We were still filming my academic work to build a portfolio. I told mom I wanted to make a video from this and post it on YouTube. I did and it went viral. I used social media to tell the world what was happening. I made a Facebook page, "I Stand with Henry" and I put the video up. Support came from people all around the world. Knowing people stood with me and believed in me helped me make it through the months of fighting with the school and taking their tests to prove I belonged in my neighborhood school. In November, I was finally "allowed" to go there. I had an aide, but she was not a communication partner. My time at this school would have been very different with a trained communication partner.

I started classes on January 23, 2013. The first year they put me in regular and advanced classes. I was not allowed to take electives and had 6 academic classes plus PE. It was exhausting. But, I passed. They did not expect this. And for 7th grade, they placed me in all Advanced Honors and Advanced Honors Gifted classes. My grades got even better, I made As and Bs. I took multiple choice tests and quizzes to show I knew the material. The advanced classes are more interesting than the regular and special education classes. It should not surprise educators that students learn more when the subject is interesting. My grades surprised and angered the same people that fought to keep me out of the school. The stress and other problems at school affected my body. I had a problem with my spleen that made me very sick. There are studies about the spleen and PTSD you can google.

I had to have surgery on my spleen. During and after surgery I hemorrhaged and my heart stopped beating because there was no blood to pass through it. I came as close to dying as a human can.

After I got out of the hospital I took classes through the Hospital Homebound program. Then, we decided to homeschool through Global Village Schools. My teachers there are the best teachers I have ever had in school.

Parents, keep searching for a way for nonspeaking people to communicate. Do not give up. Introduce your kids to other disabled people, teach them about autistic or disabled people that are changing the world. We all want role models that look like ourselves, too.

Without typing and meeting other autistic people I would not have had as many life experiences.

I was in a PSA for autism for the Autistic Self Advocacy Network, guest lectured at Princeton, received an award at the National Press Club in DC for service to the Self Advocacy Community, contributed chapters to two books, and the best was a very cool kid named Lief O'Neal (Life for Lief) chose meeting and spending time with me as his Make a Wish after he got a heart transplant. Lief is autistic and types to communicate. Lief and his family got a law passed in Oregon so autistic people cannot be denied organ transplants anymore. There are many kids just like me waiting for the chance to be part of their communities.

Teachers, we need you to believe in us and we feel it when you do not. Presuming our competence is the most important thing you can do. We do not expect you to know everything about every student because we are all different. Please work with us on accommodations so we can participate in class. We need you to see us as part of your class. We want to be part of it. When the other students see you talk to us and include us, they do the same. When you give me time to answer you on an iPad or letter board they do too. Teachers your belief in your students is more powerful than anything.

School administrators, your policies and attitudes can bring the change we need. You can create an accepting school environment that appreciates human diversity, accommodates differences and does not tolerate bullying. Everyone would benefit and would pay it forward the rest of their lives.

Are you ready to help me and my neurodivergent brothers and sisters change the world?

I Am Emma

Emma Zurcher-Long

Emma Zurcher-Long is a teenage girl living in NYC. She is a public speaker, writer and likes to sing on stage. Emma applauds those who have found, or are in the process of finding, their individual voice, as she has, through typing. Emma has had the opportunity to present at autism con-ferences and schools all over North America. Her writing has been published on her blog, Emma's Hope Book, Special Parent Magazine, HALO's 2014 edition of Voices *and the anthology,* Typed Words, Loud Voices, *edited by Amy Sequenzia and Elizabeth Grace. Emma co-directed and stars in the documentary short,* Unspoken, *which premiered at the Mill Valley Film Festival October 2017 and won the TASH Positive Image in Media 2017 award. Emma wrote the lyrics, composed the music and sings her song, "Over and Coming," now available for purchase on iTunes, Spotify, Bandcamp and others. Emma would like to continue opening people's minds to differences.*

What would you do if the whimper in your heart could not find the right words to speak? What if you couldn't control the things you felt com-pelled to say, even if you knew those who heard you would not understand? Speaking is not an accurate reflection of my intelligence. Typing is a better method for me to convey my thinking, but it is laborious and exhausting. This chapter details my communication and education journey.

Learning Through Sounds

My education started long before my numerous therapy and class-room experiences. I know this mostly through pictures and videos that

I reviewed when I was a wee little one. I responded to sounds. I knew when my mom was asking me something versus trying to teach me something based on how she sounded. In fact, I would often focus on the overall sound rather than the specific words. When my mom was having a difficult day, my clue was with how she sounded rather than her body language.

When looking at a book I found it confusing because I was being taught and questioned many times in one setting and my voice-deciphering became weaker. Mom would try to point out a color to teach on one page and then question what I saw on the next page. The sound of her voice was similar and I had more difficulty recognizing the upward tone of the question. There were some words that I focused on, but many times I heard a mixture of sounds that I sometimes tried to reproduce, like, "Addada" which meant, "I'm all done."

I was trying to make sense of everything around me by sounds. New people would either be extremely interesting or irritating to me as I was introduced and familiarized myself with how they sounded. Realizing that I was spoken to again when I tried to speak was also something that I learned.

When I was asked what I wanted to wear, I would pick the second choice, since I focused on what was said last. I always had opinions, but did not know how to successfully let them be known since other things got in the way. I picked and repeated what was said last even if it was not correct or was not what I wanted. Something in me had to do that. When I got upset after making an incorrect choice, this was why.

My focusing differs, I think, from neuro-typicals. In spite of my obsessive mind, I've managed to move forward and force myself to hear other words and tones. I get the idea of many things even if I don't hear every single word. I do have days when I am struggling more, but doesn't everyone have off days?

Processing Words

When certain words trigger me, it's hard for me to do what is being asked or respond properly. It can happen many hundreds of times a day. My responses always depend on the situation and what else is going on with me and in my environment. Sometimes a word or phrase stands out, causing me anxiety or joy, and then I repeat it over and again with my inner and outer voices. Hair, for instance. I love my hair and like it best worn long and straight. I become consumed when I know that I am going to get my hair done. If someone else mentions the word hair, I hear it loudly. I can find a liking to the word "red" and can hear if anyone around me says it. Also, if you say another color during this heightened phase, I may blurt out something with the word red in it, "Red scarf!" I might say, and that will confuse people. I fully understand the spectrum of colors, but red has greater meaning to me than blue, simply because I like the color red best.

A while ago when trying to decide on a research topic for my High School Research & Writing class, I knew that it needed to be a topic that moved me, but I got lost for some time repeating the word "research" followed by a string of words that begin with "re": remember, recall, revise, repeat, reenact, rejuvenate. I don't know the length of time, but I know I felt some stress knowing the topic I chose needed to be important and listing the other words countered some of that stress.

"What's your name?" someone might ask. It's a simple question, but when I try to make the sounds that form my name, other words push and shove their way forward. Instead, "you may not spit," or "Rosie's not here!" are examples of seemingly random nonsensical, declarations that come out of my mouth. I call these utterances my "mouth words." They could be seen as traitors, belligerent bullies who seek the spotlight, but they are not. My mouth words are funny to me, but misunderstood by others. My typed words are hard for me, but understood by many. Mouth words are witty accomplices to a mind that speaks a different language entirely. There are no words, but instead a beautiful environment where feelings, sensations, colors and sounds coexist.

Welcome to Circle Time

My earliest memories of school begin with circle time. While there is something satisfying about the same structure of circle time in my experience it did not teach much. Identifying shapes was common and something we did over and over. Why is it never a different shape? Does this say something about our openness in classrooms? I was asked to find the picture that represented the weather when I was three years old through nine years old. That's a lot of years doing a similar task that involves no creativity. It did not help me dress for the appropriate weather condition and was not useful. If it was snowing I could see it and feel it. I would get distracted because I was bored. There are many times I wish I could say, "Enough of this circle time!" But instead I resorted to biting myself or blurting out something unrelated.

When I heard the same requests repeated, I thought that maybe I was invisible or a ghost. I would play games with myself to entertain. One therapist had lipstick on her tooth and all I could concentrate on was the red tooth. I matched the pictures incorrectly because all I saw was a red tooth on every card. They probably called that a fail even though I knew very well what a cat was.

It was comical how teachers talked to one another, oblivious to the fact that their students were not aliens. In other words, I could hear and understand everything they said. When I fidgeted with my favorite string repeatedly, the teachers would say, "Put that string in Emma's bag so she does not see it." It was so loud that the voice rang and repeated in both of my ears. I then wanted to figure out where in the bag it was although my body did not seek out the bag. When other students walked past my bag I shouted their name. I was hoping one of the teachers would see this pattern, but no. You might think I was always frustrated or upset, but I was not. It became an experiment. If, and when, clues were discovered, the challenge was that my consistency fluctuated. For example, I may have missed calling the student's name who was close to my bag due to other environmental or mental distractions. I must note that these were select teachers and not all.

The phrase, "Go home" caused problems for me in school. I felt that it was personal to me. When teachers would say it while talking to other teachers, or students, and then no action was taken with me, it was upsetting and I would yell. The teachers didn't understand what sparked my outburst and I could not explain.

My Communication Journey

Imagine for a minute that you can't talk to people in any way that makes sense to them. Imagine if every time you opened your mouth to speak, other words tumbled out. If you are like me, you might get used to not answering people's questions or being able to stay on topic. So what would you do? How would you interact with people? Would you ignore their questions? Pretend you didn't hear them? How would you express yourself? Maybe you would try to connect with scripts you've memorized, things you've heard other people say in similar situations or maybe you'd find non-word based ways to communicate. That's what I do.

When I typed for the first time, and the words I typed were read aloud, the sensation cannot be fully described in words. My focus became present and I was functioning in real time. My fingers had a purpose I had not known before. It was the closest that my communication had ever come to matching the thoughts in my brain. I was heard in a new way and everything changed. My mom and dad were both speechless and had so much to say simultaneously. I felt like I was talking inside of a tunnel and there was no question whether or not I was heard. The echo was beautiful as I heard Mom telling others.

Until the moment I typed to communicate, time had a different meaning. Past and future were more familiar to me as I was constantly trying to be understood. My behavior let people know that something may have happened that upset me, and effort was spent trying to figure it out. In a similar manner, loved ones asked me questions to try and predict my immediate future in order to dodge potential triggers. The present was lost and I only noticed it when I began to type. Real time reactions were new to me. I was being validated based on what I spelled and typed rather than based on my behavior. I tried out different things because I could and wanted to experience a person's in-the-moment reaction.

When I was twelve-years-old I typed that I wanted to be a female magician. It was fun to witness the immediate support even though I wasn't sure that career was for me. That moment I felt as though I could do anything. Mom and Dad took it seriously and were excited. There was something magical about this new way of being heard. I was exposed and while many times it was freeing I didn't feel the need to always be exposed. My mind still belonged to me and I did not want to constantly peel off all the layers.

It was interesting witnessing Mom and Dad at this time, because they didn't know if typing should be all day, every day and I was trying to figure it out also. This was new. The attention I got when I typed was intense and all focus was on me. Every single word that I typed was digested as though it was the last bite of the most delicious decadent cake. Is a full-time sugar high healthy? I love cake, but I wasn't positive this intensity needed to happen all the time. You get full after that much cake and need a break.

Typing to connect with others at school has been a slower progression. When I returned from seeing Soma the first time I was not understood any differently when I went back to school. The echo started to fade. I wondered if my life would resemble Jekyll and Hyde. I thought that I had the same face but maybe there were two. I was still the same girl. I am still the same girl. The girl who secretly ate grapes in the closet when she was put on that gluten free, casein free diet. The girl who held a string. The girl who spoke random words that seemed not to make sense. This girl had the same heart and the same soul. She was just understood differently. She found comfort in her words being validated yet was cautious about being fully exposed. My brain took pictures of people's reactions to my typing and pictures tell a lot. My brain stores more information than the number of books at The Strand (a bookstore). I am now believing that people do see me differently but I am very much the same person.

What I did realize was that I found a new respect for those who took my typed words seriously. That was the biggest issue with my school at the time. They seemed to have ignored this new realization and continued speaking to me as if I retained very little. Even today, I haven't changed all that much.

Inclusive Schooling

Today I am included in some classes that are above my grade level and I am excelling. Thanks to technology I also take classes online. My schedule is full with added creative classes. The road to get here had some icy patches and some street cones were knocked down along the way. I take seriously what's expected of me even if it doesn't always appear that way. As I have gotten older, my mind has expanded and my maturity has risen. It takes a great deal of energy to compete with my obsessive mind, so I try to save the competition for select parts of my day, such as my classes. When I'm walking around outside, I usually let myself be free.

Being in a class full of neurotypical teens for the first time was incredible. I watched carefully how they dressed and acted. I was treated kindly, though I had difficulty staying as composed as my classmates. I wanted to show everyone I had a smart mind and I only hoped that I would not get kicked out for being disruptive.

I am better understood now even when I'm not typing. I find that my parents know my capabilities and so the overall way of life has changed. The frustrations are still present, but their minds have expanded and take me more seriously. My atypical brain now leads an atypical daily life. I spend less hours in school, but I am challenged more as I am enrolled in select high school courses. I went from circle time to writing a thesis. I went from special education to regular education. I went from being told most things, to being asked. What gets me thinking sometimes is what my future is going to look like. Is college the right path for me? Will I work for someone or be an entrepreneur? What will my life look like socially? How will the world change to accept differences? I can find excitement in the bigger unknowns of life even when schedule changes of daily life can bring me anxiety.

So what is to be done with someone like me? Is it better to put students like myself, of which there are many, in segregated schools or classrooms, is inclusion the better option, or is there another answer? I was believed not capable enough to attend a regular school, nor was I able to prove this assumption wrong. In an ideal world these questions would not need to be asked because a diagnosis of autism would not lead to branding a person as less than or inferior. Those who cannot speak or who have limited speech would not immediately be labeled "intellectually disabled" and "low functioning." We would live in a society that would embrace diversity and welcome all people, regardless of race, culture, religion, neurology or disability. Our education system mirrors our society and in both, we come up short.

In New York City, kids like me are not attending mainstream schools because we are believed to be unable to learn complex subject matter. I was sent to both public and private special education schools, specifically created for speaking and non-speaking autistic students and those believed to have emotional issues. Because I cannot voice my thoughts and so rely on favorite scripts, my spoken language causes people to assume my thinking is simple, I am unable to pay attention and cannot comprehend most of what is said to me.

As a result, none of these schools presumed that I, or the other students, were competent and their curricula reflected this. At the private school I attended for six years, I was regularly asked to do simple equations such as $3 + 2 = $ _____.

When I said "two," because that was the last number spoken and my mouth would not form the word "five," my teachers believed I could not do basic math. It was the same with reading, and something as simple as being asked to define the word "cup."

I clearly know what a cup is, but when I could not say it, I was marked as not knowing. This school used the same fairy tale, "Three Billy Goats Gruff," for three years as the foundation of a "curriculum." At another school, this time public, while my older brother was learning about World War II and writing essays on whether the United States should have dropped an atomic bomb on Hiroshima, my class was planting seeds in soil and asked what kinds of things were needed for the seed to take root and grow.

When my classmates, many of whom could not speak at all, and I could not answer with the words "sunlight" and "water," it was assumed we did not know the answers or understand the question. At another public school I spent months going over how many seconds are in a minute, minutes in an hour, hours in a day, but when I could not demonstrate that I understood either in writing or spoken language, it was believed I had no concept of time.

There is no test that allows me to show the creative ways in which I learn. I cannot sit quietly unless I am able to twirl my string, softly murmur to myself and have a timer nearby. I cannot read aloud or answer most questions verbally, but I can type. My mind is lightning fast. I can hear a song and then replay it note for note with my voice. I have an incredibly large capacity to listen, learn and feel. I listen to conversations around me regularly and often wish that some parents would appreciate their children more.

The other day on the subway a Mom said, "Shut up, you're being stupid!" to her son. The boy was silent and put his head down. The Mom proceeded to play a game on her phone. I have learned that everyone is delicate. In that moment my body felt tremendous sadness.

I see patterns in unrelated things, such as I am able to notice every article of clothing that someone wears on a given day. People's attitudes are reflected in their choice of clothing. When the same clothes are worn over and over, I have the feeling the wearer is stuck. People's self-confidence increases when wearing new clothing.

My expansive vocabulary is impressive. I've listened to how people put words together my entire life. As I have made sense of the words used, I have been able to understand their meaning, though I am unable to ask for definitions. I notice people's sadness, even when they are smiling. I almost feel like I am violating someone because I can see inside of them and know their feelings. I'm told I use the written word in unusual and interesting ways. I have been published in magazines and blogs. I give presentations around the country on autism and recently gave the keynote address at an autism conference. I co-directed a documentary, *Unspoken*, about my life and being autistic and I hope, one day, to be a performer, but reserve the right to change my mind about this career choice.

My ideal school: I would like to not be the only student who types to speak. I would not want to go back to being in the same environment all day. The variety of my surroundings is important. Exploratory excursions feed my brain and are therefore essential to my learning. The best education I've received to date in a school is at a private non-special education school, where none of the teachers or administration has been given "training" in autism or what that supposedly means. They do not believe I cannot do things the other students are able to do. In fact, though I am just fifteen-years old and technically should be a freshman, I am doing work designated for a grade higher.

I am treated respectfully by teachers and students alike. My typing is slow, but the class waits for me and gives me a chance to express myself. During a Socratic seminar in my Freshman year where the students were expected to speak on the book we had just finished, everyone waited for me to type my thoughts and gave me time to have my thoughts on an earlier point, read later. In my theater class the teacher began the semester with non-speaking work. We learned about mime, silent theater and the importance and impact of physicality while performing. I have been asked for what I need in order to excel, and accommodations have been made, I know, but I hope and believe that I am not the only one benefiting from my presence at such a terrific school.

The Autistic Mind

I often think if all humans could experience the world in hi-res, technicolor, surround sound as I do, everyone would be happier. I have come to understand that my mind is not like most people's. I am Autistic.

Many people believe autism describes a simple mind, and that someone like me has no understanding or awareness of my surroundings. My hearing is excellent. Things like the honking noise made by impatient drivers who think the sound of their horn will miraculously clear the road ahead is so intense I can become lost in the key of their horn. I am compelled to imitate each one I hear. Car horns I can respond to cheerfully. It's the same with light. The harshness coupled with bloated heavy air is so intense I become overwhelmed. I wonder if I am too aware of my surroundings.

Some people have suggested I am unable to feel empathy and assume I have no desire for human interaction and friendship. I feel people's intentions and feelings so intensely it can be difficult to concentrate. I am too sensitive to other people's sadness; it is akin to drowning or like being smothered by the weight of damp earth covering your entire body, filling your eyes, mouth and ears. Piercing shards of past and present pain cause me to turn away or make faces or laugh out loud to lessen the weightiness. There is no lack of empathy, but rather an unmanageable abundance that defies my best intentions.

It is during these moments that I flounder because society expects less of me and not more. I listen to the words spoken by people who are crying or shouting. They say things like, "I'm okay," through tears or "No, I'm not angry," as they clench their fists, but their words are in direct conflict with their actions.

Others believe that I do not have feelings at all. How do you defend yourself against such accusations? Trying to convince those who believe

I'm an empty shell is impossible. Adding to this is my inability to use spoken language as expected.

"No, you cannot put putty in your mouth!" in answer to "what's wrong with that girl who is crying in the corner?" does not help change the minds of those who believe me incompetent and without feelings.

If I tell my mouth to behave and demand that certain words come out, stress barks and growls, jarring my mind so that it folds in on itself and favorite scripts begin. "You cannot throw your lunchbox at Kevin!" or "Maddie's not here anymore!" helps me control the waves of anxiety that press up against me. Hearing my voice keeps the dark, piercing void of nothingness from engulfing me. My brain doesn't think in words the way most people's do. Names of things and people get handed to me instead of the words that would make sense to the person questioning me. Sometimes I blurt out whole sentences from another time in my life. They may be images that remind me of the person I'm with or where I am, or words I've heard spoken by others, things that get caught in my mind, or unrelated scripts, but that convey the exact emotion I'm feeling. In any case, what I manage to say usually baffles the people I am speaking to, causing them to misunderstand me. Not being able to speak what's in my heart so that others are able to understand can be challenging, but usually I can type things that I cannot reliably say.

Clenching down on my forearm as hard as I can is another way to control the tidal wave of stress. A complete set of teeth marks embedded into my skin might interest those in the field of dentistry, but for most people witnessing, horror probably best describes their response. Some find self-injury baffling, even terrifying and something that must be stopped at all costs, even if this means far more painful interventions inflicted by others than anything I could do to myself. I see it as a way to care for and acknowledge the overwhelming onslaught of unruly feelings.

This perception is not understood by "autism experts" who use words like "behaviors," "defiant," and "oppositional" to defend the use of isolation rooms, restraints and even electric shocks for people like me. It seems abuse by others to prevent self-injury is permitted, even applauded, though the logic is lost on me. When my mind is caught in a downward spiral, I need calm reassurance.

My frustration often expressed in screaming, repetitive scripts grind down the patience of those witnessing. My screams threaten their kindness, I know, but I cannot stop once begun and pounding terror is all that remains. Only the dedicated few talk of love during my episodes of furious stress and suffering. Their love is a rejuvenate force and restores my faith in this awkward world.

I am exuberant, overflowing with energy. I'd rather gallop than walk, bounce than sit quietly. I'm happiest with high volume, intense beats, jumping, arms flailing, pounding bass, total darkness or bright stage lights and a microphone in hand. I want people to hear me. I am as versed in making silly faces as I am in my favorite songs and my neurology. My mind is lightning fast, hungry, logical. I'm a seeker, determined, a lover of laughter in a body trying to keep up. It can't, but I'll keep trying.

Showing kindness toward those who are different and embracing our imperfections as proof of our humanness is the remedy for fear. Love is a small word, but allow yourself to be consumed by the sensation and the world becomes a place of infinite possibility. I want my hard won words to give hope and inspire people to change how they think about autism and someone like me.

The Power of Music

Sound is everywhere. I don't have a filtering system marking one particular sound as more important than another. My brain doesn't do that. It hears all sounds equally and does not discriminate. But some people's voices are not as dramatic to my ear as the honking of a horn. I love the sound of honking horns. Favoring some sounds dilutes others, but music has the best sounds of all. Music is my first language. It is a friend who loves me unconditionally. It's there when I need it and does not shed a tear if ignored for some time. Music is a positive force as it stands by my side. I like hearing the same melodies repeated and did even when I was very young. It's been a comfort to me as long as I can remember. Music grounds me and plays a huge role in seeking my creativity as it allows me to perform as I choose to. It's a way to communicate; it gives me hope, tells me I am not alone and inspires me to create. Though people respond differently to music, I believe there are always emotions involved. Music has the ability to transform my fearsome thoughts laden with anxiety and stress. It calms me and this has been the case throughout my life. When singing lyrics I stumble and have trouble articulating the words, but I can remember the sounds I hear and recreate them with my voice.

When I sing I am not apart from, but instead am part of. I like the idea of being a performer, though I am not positive that I can do it. When my body is out of sync, I think it might be difficult.

Music can be both private and public, but it needs to be loud. No one composes music in a whisper. My body needs to feel the beat so that I can be consumed by it. When that happens I become part of the music, like another instrument or an extension of it. I jump and dance and move. My arms swing or are raised up and my head bops, my whole body keeps time to the beat. I'm transported to another reality and it is in this alternate reality that I am most happy and comfortable.

At home, my need for high volume can cause problems because the members of my family have differing sensory needs that come in direct conflict with mine. My older brother has to have music as background, while I perform alongside, so it makes sense for mine to be public and his to be private.

My mom and dad both work at home and need quiet in order to concentrate. I am told to wear headphones, which encumber my movement and dilute my experience. My family has worked out a solution that allows me to commandeer the living room in the evening. For several hours I am blissfully able to indulge my love of loud music and dancing while my brother stays in his room or hangs out with my parents in theirs.

Until a few years ago I didn't know the joy of creating music. Until then I was an audience member, but not a participant. My parents encouraged my love of music and hired teachers to help me expand my interests. Guitar is beautiful to listen to, but it is difficult for my fingers to recreate the sounds flowing through my mind. Piano is also hard and requires dedication and lots of practice, but I think it's a better fit for me. Singing is easy and my lack of inhibitions, great sense of tone and ability to mimic sounds I hear makes it the best choice of all.

Eliot is my piano teacher and Karen is my singing coach. Karen and I have great fun together. I feel at ease in her presence, which is important when you are learning new things and trying to be creative. Eliot and Karen have taught me to be patient with myself. From them I have learned how hard it is to become masterful and yet I've decided it's better to love the process of learning as much as the final product. Communicating isn't just talking, it's developing a connection with another.

The Future for Students Like Me

Every time I type in front of new people I am advocating for myself. I always wonder if their response to me will be sincere. Conferences are filled with many believers and it feels good to get the praise. I want people to know I am vibrant. I am funny. I am wise. I am smart. I have a large imagination and I love creative arts. I have a loud voice even when I am in a quiet mood and my body is not always gentle. I wish to be happy.

I worry about the future of autistic people who type. I wonder if there will be any advancement with research. I hope that there will be more inclusion and acceptance that autism does not automatically mean—can't, won't, or doesn't. There is a saying in the disabilities community, "Nothing about us, without us." A complete rethinking about autism and autistic neurology is needed if special education schools or any schools are going to educate those of us who think differently. Believing in the potential of all students is not on any test. The presumption that each and every student, whether they can speak or not, can and will eventually learn given the necessary supports and encouragement is not common, but it should be. I hope that [other people who type to communicate] won't be questioned and they will have plenty of people to communicate with in the same fashion. With all students it's crucial to be open to their potential. I can add that the student needs to be in a comfortable environment and also be challenged. The equation should be ideal for a successful learning experience.

Wouldn't it be great if autistic people's ideas were included in designing curriculum and the tests that are meant to evaluate them? Isn't that what you would want if you were like me?

9

Write to Be Heard

Philip Reyes

Philip Reyes is a high school junior and aspiring writer. He has a blog, "Faith, Hope, and Love with Autism." Philip's writings have been featured in The Buffalo News, Parents Magazine, The Mighty, Golden Hat Foundation, *and* Typed Words, Loud Voices. *His interests include bike riding, learning about history, teaching others about autism, and advocating for effective communication. Philip thanks his mom, Lisa, for being his constant help and encouragement. She supported Philip in writing this chapter. "I love you, mom." You can follow Philip's blog at www. faithhopeloveautism.blogspot.com*

Silence

My name is Philip. I am 16 years old. I am writing to talk about how communication opened up the world to me. I did not always have a means to express myself. I am autistic and nonspeaking. For many years I led a silent life. I had many thoughts and things I wanted to say. But my mouth would not move at my mind's command. I only learned to express myself purposefully at age 9 when I learned Rapid Prompting Method (RPM) from Soma Mukhopadhyay.

I lived in Miami, Florida when I was younger. Every day I enjoyed sunny days. I loved to walk outside. I would study the cars, the boundaries between the grass and sidewalk, the street signs, and the sky. When I was young, mom sang to me a lot. She sang to teach me about the world. She sang to make me interact with her. She tried to get me to

143

talk by leaving the end of the verse blank and waiting for me to finish it. I tried my best but I could not get my words out. I eventually could make sounds similar to the words. It was the music that seemed to make my body be more calm and better able to cooperate. My first words came out this way. They were "star" and "are" to the song Twinkle Twinkle. This is how I came to love music.

I began to hear people worrying about me. I saw my parents' concerned faces. I learned I could not do the same things my siblings could do at my age. They thought I might be "slow" or hard of hearing. I was neither, but no one knew I was in a body that didn't follow my mind's commands. I wanted a different body that would allow me to move and talk the way I wanted to. I learned I had autism when I was 2 and three-quarters. I was sad when I got diagnosed because everyone cried like I had died. I was not dead. I was still here. But everyone became sad about me.

I started Early Intervention School. My teacher was Miss C. She sang to me all the time. I loved going there. Miss C greeted me every day with a "Hello Philip" song. We ate breakfast. I learned to feed myself. I also had circle time and work time with my classmates. I was there only one year.

When I was almost 3 I started applied behavior analysis (ABA) when I got home from school. I had several high school and college helpers. They would sit at a table with me and do flashcard drills with me. I had to point to the card with the picture they said. Then I started matching. I also started to talk. At first it was to request food. I was happy I could talk. I appreciated the power it gave me. Later I could label items on flashcards. I really began to think I might be able to talk like everyone else. ABA was fun at the beginning. I was challenged to do things I could not do before. However, after about a year of ABA, I still could not talk the way I wanted to. I heard my thoughts clearly, but my mouth said something else like tickle or milk. I was frustrated ABA could not succeed in helping me communicate.

I started to resent my ABA programs. Too much emphasis was made on making rote responses to very basic concepts. I felt like I was being trained like a pet. I became increasingly frustrated. My days were filled with matching flashcards and following pointless commands. I began to act more aggressively towards my teachers. I did not care about how I answered. I felt trapped in preschool year after year. This felt like prison with no hope for getting out.

When I was nine-and-a-half, I went to my first bike camp. I did not succeed in learning to ride a bike yet. But my mom met Mrs. Carson. Her son Matthew was in my camp. Matthew is a few years older than me. He too is nonspeaking. He was able to communicate with a letter board. My mom was impressed. She asked Mrs. Carson how Matthew had learned. Mom learned that they did Rapid Prompting Method (RPM). She decided RPM was what I needed.

New Possibilities

When I was 9 and a half I went to Austin, Texas to meet Soma Mukhopadhyay to learn RPM. I was excited about traveling with my parents but I was nervous I would not be able to succeed at the new therapy. I was used to failing to meet expectations. I hoped my parents would not be disappointed. When I met Soma, she immediately started talking to me. "The sky is blue. What did I say?" she asked. "The sky is blue or the sky is green." She had me pick from written words instead of pictures. I knew how to read. She knew I could. Soma also taught me lessons that were interesting. I learned about pilgrims, the water cycle, math, and fables. I even got to show my parents I could spell well. I answered many questions. I enjoyed it so much. I was happy Soma believed in me. I was amazed I could show what I knew with Soma. I could succeed with Soma in a way that I could not with others because Soma knew I needed to be treated intelligently to respond. She gave me a way to respond intelligently through spelling. It was the first time I was able to clearly express what I was really thinking. My mom and dad cried. They never knew I was smart. My trip to Austin was the best moment in my life. I wanted to stay in Austin forever. Mom and Dad also made me feel special. I got all their attention. My siblings usually get the attention for their accomplishments. They are good at sports. I have always gone to their competitions. This time it was all about me. I loved having my parents' attention as we looked around Austin and played at the playground. Making quality time for me made me feel so loved. My time in Austin was the best experience.

When I came home, I was sad not to be able to respond to my parents like I did with Soma. I could not move my body in the way I wanted yet. I was not used to mom teaching me. I did not know if she would be able to do it. Soma knew how to prompt me to move my body to respond. Mom did not prompt me enough so I would get distracted with everything else and respond more randomly. I think we frustrated each other a lot in the beginning. I wanted her to quit at times when she yelled at me for being unable to respond correctly. She did not know I could get the right answers in my head but could not express it yet. I am glad mom persisted and never gave up. At first mom taught me from science and American history workbooks. She also went to the library to get me books on holidays and biographies.

Learning new things made my mind expand. I loved finding out about famous people like Frederick Douglass and Malala. Their stories inspired me to work hard to learn and write my words. Eventually I began to get better at controlling my finger to point accurately. I could spell well enough and start using my skills to communicate. I was ready to talk. Once I could spell to talk, I began telling my mom about autism and how I experience it. I loved to talk about autism because I could finally make people understand me. I started to believe I could help more people. Like the way Frederick Douglass helped fellow slaves obtain freedom by his story, I might be able to set my autistic brothers and sisters free from silence with the telling of my story.

My mom and I started a blog. She named it "Faith, Hope, and Love with Autism." I liked that she was sharing my successes. Many people started reading it. Mom would tell me the different countries our readers came from. People from all the continents of the world read it. My mom began to get better at helping me express myself by giving me topics to write about. I would write about different holidays, lessons mom taught, things in the news, and eventually my perceptions on autism. I began to see how I could make a difference through writing. Talking through the Internet gave my words power by reaching many people at once. I only had to tell it once and it was like talking to a hundred people. I especially liked when people commented. Blogging has been the closest thing to having conversations with people.

Educational Transition

At home I was learning many interesting things but at school I was still learning basic counting and flashcard drills. I went to an ABA school with a good reputation. However, I was so bored there. I started to care about learning more than what I was able to get from my ABA school. Mom tried to encourage my school to raise the level of my work and use the letterboard but they never tried. I began to get mad at my teachers for denying me my letterboard at ABA school. I wanted so badly to be able to show people I could learn more.

Mom finally decided to get me into Heim, the public middle school, after many failed attempts to get my ABA school to teach me more grade level academics. I knew I had to leave when the staff said they would never try to learn how to do RPM or use the letterboard. When I was almost 11, Heim accepted me in the middle of the year. Heim already had Matthew there so I was fortunate they already knew how to use the letterboard and presume my intelligence. I was so happy I was going to get a more advanced education but I was so nervous about fitting in. All my life I had gone to special education and never mingled with neurotypical kids. I knew my autistic actions like moving, vocalizing, and stimming were my biggest obstacles.

Before I went to Heim, mom taught me about Moses. God chose Moses to lead the Israelites out of slavery in Egypt. But Moses was scared to be a leader because he didn't speak well. Moses tried to get God to choose someone else but God would not. God listened to Moses' pleas and gave him a helper. He sent Aaron to be the spoken voice of Moses' thoughts. I saw myself as being like Moses, but I was escaping meaningless time in a school that taught me preschool material year after year. I was ready to be free to learn new things and bring my autistic classmates on the freedom trail with me. Although I was excited, I was fearful I would not do a good job. I asked God to help me like Moses. I prayed I could control my body enough to be able to spell on my letterboard with my new teachers.

I visited the class at Heim before I started. This class was an autism class that was more like a regular academic classroom. Mom told me that some kids get to take regular classes if they are able to do the work. I learned Mr. Bradley would be my teacher in the autism class. I hoped he would be nice and treat me normally. When I first met Mr. Bradley I liked him. Mr. Bradley greeted me like a regular kid. He didn't talk in baby language or over-exaggerated fluctuation in tones. I talked to him on my letterboard. I told him I do not need to work for candy. I didn't need edible reinforcers to learn. I just wanted to learn new and interesting things like most kids do. Visiting Heim helped me prepare myself to get excited about starting school there.

I began at Heim in February 2014. I meant to show everyone at school how I communicate by spelling on my letterboard. I was ready to show everyone how smart I was. I learned that acting smart would be a challenge. I lacked the ability to make my body calm. I was constantly running out of my seat. I could not stop myself from moving. The more I moved, the more anxious I got. I was constantly at war with my body. I struggled keeping my body from doing disruptive actions like throwing myself on the ground or yelling out loud. I had many meltdowns my first month at school. I feared I might never get myself under control to spell with my teachers. I gave my teachers lots of practice to persevere through my difficult times.

Despite my difficulties the first month, I loved going to Heim. Mr. Bradley already had a student like me. He already believed I could understand everything I was taught. But my first two years at Heim were spent mostly in the autism class. My exposure to neurotypical students came in homeroom, specials, and lunch. I wanted to be in regular classes but my quest to go was halted by my uncooperative body. I had to learn to be more calm. The autism class was better than my old school. Mr. Bradley taught English and Language Arts (ELA) and math. It was more advanced than the picture recognition and counting I did at my old school. In ELA we learned about current events from Newsela, a newspaper for students. We answered comprehension questions. In math we did real life math problems like buying and making change. It was great to learn more than I learned before at school, but I still longed to take the courses my neurotypical classmates took. Over time I improved greatly in communicating and spelling with Mr. Bradley, my speech teacher Ms. Martin, and many of my aides. My time in the autism class prepared me to type and regulate my body for regular class. I started to become restless about waiting for my chance to go to regular classes.

During my first 2 years at Heim I worked on my blog a lot to educate my teachers, classmates, and readers about me. I wanted people to understand me. Blogging helped me by giving me a voice so others could know me. Being known by my words instead of by my behaviors has made me more peaceful in my soul.

I wrote a letter to my classmates. These were neurotypical classmates in my homeroom. My teacher read the letter out loud for me.

Dear Classmates,

My name is Philip. I am almost eleven. I want you to know I spell on my letterboard to communicate. The reason is I am autistic and cannot talk. I can like the same things today as you do. I am very smart but my body is dumb. My body will not listen to my brain. I may want to say, "Hi, how are you?" but it comes out wrong. I have some interests. I like to watch soccer and TV. I like to listen to music and read biographies. I am pretty shy to play with other kids. I am wanting you to simply understand who I am. I have feelings like you. I'm telling you to consider me as none other than like you. Someday I hope to talk too. I am understanding lonely, rightly so. I am one to understand someone's beliefs about me. I look dumb, sorry, and fearful. I hope to change your perceptions. I am someone who has to work so hard to get by in this world. I am kind of built for another planet. To understand this, please do not tease me. I kind of feel bad when you sometimes ignore me. It sometimes makes me feel like I don't matter. Even if I look like I don't like you, I do. I might make a lot of noise because sometimes I can't help it. I reach out to you so we can be friends. Thank you for listening.

Sincerely,
Philip

Everyone listened quietly and arranged their focus on me. I felt peaceful and more understood after it was read. My classmates talked more to me after. I learned to relax more. I was preparing myself to help my school understand me so I could be included.

In my 6th grade year, my friend Kaylie joined my class. Kaylie learned to type through RPM too. I liked having Kaylie in my class because I was losing my autistic friend Matthew, who was graduating and moving on to high school. Kaylie and I pushed each other to get better at our communication skills. That year we both moved from using letterboards to Bluetooth keyboards. I loved being able to work on an iPad to show my work. Kaylie and I grew closer that year. We were often paired for speech and math. Kaylie made me eager to work hard because I did not want to look like the dumber one. I tried harder to sit better. My teachers got better supporting me. I did especially well typing with

Ms. Martin. She was the speech therapist and she was the first to really get the hang of it with me. I loved typing with Ms. Martin. I could tell her a lot and she made me feel very smart and interesting to be around.

Around the spring of 6th grade, I was tired of waiting to get a chance to take regular classes. My mom wrote my teachers often about letting me sit in regular science. I finally got to try going to science as an observer the last few months. I loved the interesting things I learned. I wanted to make sure I could keep going next year. My Individualized Education Program (IEP)assessment was coming soon. Mom had me prepare a statement for the committee in advance. I wrote:

> Dear Committee,
>
> I ask you to please consider me for regular academic classes. I am a smart boy and want to be challenged. A most desired goal of mine is to get a high school diploma. I want to use my mind in a career in journalism and writing. Good education helps me maintain my mind and grow as a person. I love you to learn from me too. May I be a part of regular classes to teach classmates about autism? I am a good learner and teacher. I am making progress everyday with my skills. I try to meet peace in my life so I can meet my goals. Leaving stims behind is much work, but I am determined to try. No matter what, I am determined to succeed. Please help me reach my goals.
>
> Thank you,
Philip

Mom was upset when Mr. Bradley called the day before my IEP saying I was not ready for regular classes. I felt betrayed because he kept telling me I was improving so much. I wanted my chance to finally be educated like most kids my age. I wanted this so badly. Mom asked if I would like to appear before the committee myself. She thought I would convince the committee better if I came in person. On the day of my IEP I went to school nervous but excited. I practiced what I wanted to say in my head all night. I prayed God would bless me and make the committee like me enough to let me in regular science for 7th grade. When I got to the meeting, everyone was already there. There were probably 10 people sitting around a big table. People smiled at me as I took my place at the head of the table with my iPad. Mom held my keyboard. Someone asked me, "How could we help you the best?" I typed, "Give me regular education." The head of the committee asked what my favorite class was. I told her science. My homeroom teacher asked how

I liked the science classes I sat in on. I told him I loved it. After some consideration and discussion, the head said I should have a chance to go to regular classes next year. I was so happy. I was able to speak for myself. I was able to convince people to give me a chance. I was ready to prove they made the right decision. I thanked God for answering my prayers.

Inclusion

I started 7th grade attending regular science and social studies. I continued to take ELA and math with the autism class. My regular classes were so interesting. I learned about the body and U.S. history up to the Civil War. I learned more in one year than in all my previous school years in special education combined. I loved it. However, I still could not type with my main aide very well. I did not do well on my tests. I meant to be able to type my answers but I was given choices in a way I could not get myself to perform accurately. I learned to type with everyone else though. Perhaps I made more progress with some people more than others because they were more confident in my ability and more at peace working with me. Mr. Bradley got really good at working with me. He made the subjects in his class more challenging by teaching the topics at different levels. Kaylie and I got the most challenging questions to answer. By the time I finished 7th grade, Mr. Bradley and I had gotten the hang of each other. He knew what helped me best and I became comfortable typing with him. I could type sentences with him this year compared to just single words last year.

I started making friends in regular classes. Learning to interact socially is still a big challenge, but I have been able to make friends in my own way. My friends give me questions on index cards and I answer them on my own time. It has been nice to be noticed and included. People think I am interesting. I am not what they expected. I like that my classmates talk normally to me. They try to include me as an equal. Here are some of the conversations I have had with my classmates.

From C:

(1) What is it like not being able to communicate with people?
(2) What is it like having no control over your body?

My responses:

(1) I am better now that I can type. People who can't communicate are sad. I used to get angry mom could not make me talk. I made many imaginary friends. Not being able to talk is really frustrating. I think fast but my mouth can't say the words. I pass the time writing the thoughts in my mind. I am practicing what I would say. Peace came to me when I started to spell my thoughts. I am talking now (through typing) and it feels peaceful to know people can understand me.

(2) Having little control of my body is maddening. I am always getting lost in outer space. I feel like there is no gravity. My body has little mass. I have to concentrate hard to move purposely and slowly. Even typing takes patience and precision. It is hard work for me.

A wrote:

Hi Philip,

I just wanted to ask how you are taught or how you learn to speak sign language. It seems hard to learn so I want to know how you learn it. Also, how long did it take to learn what you know now?

My response:

I do not know sign. I type my answers. My method of communication is Rapid Prompting Method. I learned when I was nine. I started by going to Austin, Texas to learn from Soma how to learn about lessons for kids my age. I was given lessons in math, science, history, and literature for the first time. My parents learned to teach me. I talked by pointing to letters on a letterboard to spell words. Later I learned to type. I still need an aide to help me stay focused and on task. This is because autism makes me captive to impulses. An aide helps me overcome my impulses so I can follow where my mind really wants to go. A lot of practice has gotten me far. I still have a long way to go. People make my life better by politely helping me be peacefully included. I am always treated well at Heim.

From M:

Dear Philip,

I have some questions to ask you. First, what does your brain think about when you do things like watch TV, and if you understand movies, what is your favorite movie? Second, how and when did you get diagnosed with autism? Finally, is there a way you can climb over autism and speak your mind like neurotypical people?

From Me:

> When I watch TV, my brain often loses its peace. For me, the moving pictures and loud noise is too much for me to take in all at once. I practice watching TV by either looking out of the side of my eyes to limit the visual input or I just listen. I like movies because of the good stories. My favorite movie is Big Hero 6. I liked that the main character was smart. Lots of action too. I was diagnosed with autism when I was 2 and a half. People diagnosed me because I didn't talk. I can climb over the autism wall by talking by typing because my mouth can't talk. I can look more neurotypical by practicing being with you more.

From J:

> How many different types of autism are there?

From Me:

> I think there are different autisms. People call it a spectrum. Teachers make accommodations according to our individual needs. Some autistics think in pictures like Temple Grandin. Some, like me, think in letters and words. Some autistics can talk. Others cannot. Some autistics can coordinate their movement well. Some cannot. I have a hard time with talking and movement. I have a hard time moving purposely. I pace a lot to make my body calm. Saving my manpower for meaningful tasks takes lots of concentration. People may do things differently but we all think, love, and want to be loved. Let's try persuading lots of people that autistics are really smart and friendly. I want you to accept me just like anyone else.

Through my unconventional interactions with my classmates, they learned autism was not a disease but a different way of sensing, moving, and interacting with the environment. They learned that even though I can't speak, I understand, feel, and have goals just like they do. I became more confident in myself that year.

This is my last year at Heim. Learning to be more calm all day is a challenge. I take four regular classes: science, social studies, health, and technology. I still work with Mr. Bradley in math and ELA. All my classes are very interesting. Science is still my favorite. I am preparing to transition to high school. I hear high school is hard but I want to meet the challenge of graduating with a diploma.

Ascending Toward My Potential

I have come a long way from when I was first diagnosed with autism. Many years were wasted in misunderstanding. My life was unknown to everyone until I met Soma. Soma raised the bar on my potential. Before RPM, low expectations held me back the most. I was treated like a toddler for many years. I was thought to have no intelligence because I couldn't speak. I heard people talk about me as if I were not present. Many bad things were said about me and the hardship I caused. It was torture to hear people use autism as a bad word. I am still healing from my years of being misunderstood. Those years without RPM were like being in prison without hope for freedom. RPM was the key to finally release me. Today I am free to ascend toward my God-given potential.

My quest is to help the world see the potential of autistic people like me. Peace comes with love and acceptance. To make our lives better, please begin by seeing us as smart. Don't be afraid to talk to us even if we seem uninterested. Know that my body often betrays my true feelings and intentions. My typed words are my true thoughts. Schools should be open to support people like me who can learn and participate with assistance. My school has proven it is possible. Schools also need to be willing to learn from the students. Autistic people best explain autism. The common understanding that autism is an intellectual disability is not correct. Autism is a neurological disability that affects the way I process stimuli, move, and interact with people and the environment. Autistics are human first. I am hopeful for a better future for autistics as more of us tell our stories. I am trying to help autistics be understood. Understanding us as people is the first step in leading us to a better life. I desire a happy life like you. Making a meaningful life is what makes me happy. My contribution is helping people understand autism from an insider perspective.

I Have My Voice

Rhema Russell

Rhema is 15 years old. She has a sister named Hope that she loves more than anything. She also loves her parents so much. Her best friends are named Reilly and Sydney. Her favorite subject is science followed by math. She also enjoys gymnastics and writing on her blog. To share her story with the world is a special gift and she is grateful to a faithful God. Follow Rhema on Facebook.com/rhemashope, Instagram.com/rhemas hope, or rhemashope.wordpress.com.

> to you i am a girl who found her voice
> but i am a bird who has taken to the sky.
> i am a hyena who laughs at the world.
> i am a frog who jumps for joy.
> i am an aardvark who plays all day with worms.
> i am a lion who rules the day.
> i am a giraffe standing taller than ever.
> i am free.
>
> —Rhema

Before Meaningful Communication

Do you know what it is like to not be able to speak? It is the hardest thing when you are trying to go to school. I sometimes had no ability to make my needs known to anyone. To not have a speaking voice was debilitating. I often had to scream to get attention and do things that were troublesome to my teachers.

I knew I was quite autistic when the moment happened that I understood that no one understood that I understood.

Once I had to go to the bathroom, but I could not tell them so I peed in my pants. They thought I could not be toilet trained.

Another time I had some pants that were too big and they irritated me so much that I took them off. My teacher thought I was stripping so she put them back on. This only made me more irritated, and I melted down so much that I had to be restrained.

One time I had to work on trying to learn my letters and I could not tell them that I already knew how to read. So I acted out and did not cooperate. This is something I still do. To not have a way to prove what you know is the most frustrating existence. No one knew what I had inside of my head.

Reading is hard because it hurts my so strong eyes, but I like to read because I can learn so much. I learned to read by noticing how letters worked. I was five years old. I was delighted I could read anything I wanted. No one knew I could read because I could not tell them. I read all the time even though my teachers thought I was just coloring. When I colored the papers I was reading. When I was watching TV I was reading. It did not look like it but I was reading. My motivation was to learn as much as I could even if no one knew. *Now people know.*

Math has always been easy for me. My understanding of math comes from an ability to remember what numbers sound like. Numbers have sounds that I can hear so strongly. It is so strong that I have trouble hearing anything else. It sounds like music in my ears. Numbers each have their own notes that make a beautiful song. My favorite number is seven because it sounds like lovely chimes. And my least favorite number is four because it sounds like a bad note out of tune. I love numbers because they store themselves in my helper head. They store themselves together in songs that I can remember. They make a beautiful symphony, and my helper head is happy to hear this music. I can't wait to hear more and more. I am so thankful God gave this gift to me.

One time I wanted to tell my teachers that I could do multiplication but they did not know so they gave me the same task of identifying numbers one through nine. I always got these wrong because I was so humiliated. My mind would tell me one thing, my hand would do another. For example, my mind would say the answer is five but my hand would touch nine. How frustrating this was. This only made things worse because who could believe I could do more than that? I felt hopeless everyday as I learned about how to count to ten over and over. I was so stuck.

I wish my teachers could have understood how stuck I was and given me a way to communicate beyond "I want marker." Proloquo, a communication app on the iPad, did not work for me because the pictures limited my ability to really express my thoughts. There was no way to really say what was in my heart. This was frustrating and I was not motivated to do well. I became so worried that I would be stuck with only pictures to express myself.

My teachers were so nice and understanding but they had no way to really communicate with me. I will always love my teachers for trying their best. I am not an easy student and they really wanted me to do well.

One day I learned about how my education was impacting my future. I was devastated to realize that I would not go to high school or college. This made me so mad.

Thankfully now I can say that I am not stuck anymore.

Learning to Communicate

My mother took me to Wisconsin to learn Rapid Prompting Method (RPM) from Erika Anderson when I was eleven. I don't know what prompted my mother to take me but I am so glad she did not give up on me learning to communicate in a meaningful way. As soon as we got there, I knew this would be the way I would find my voice. The teacher taught me like I was smart. And it was the first time I thought I could be freed from my silence.

I remember running into the office and grabbing markers. Erika worked with me and tried to help me focus but I was so nervous. She taught me a lesson on the Ice Age and I was surprised that she treated me like I understood. This gave me hope. I was suddenly motivated to do well.

I remember that I made a lot of mistakes but she never simplified the lessons. This was the first time that ever happened. I was truly happy because I knew this was a new chance for me to find my voice.

I was still my difficult self, but no one gave me a reinforcer like candy for doing good work. This made me happy to be treated like a normal kid. No one expected me to fail. They thought I was intelligent. This made me want to succeed more than anything.

Now I had to overcome my fears and learn to point on my stencil board. This would not be easy. To communicate this way, I had to learn how to make my finger point to the letters inside my head. This is harder than it sounds because I have so much trouble with my motor skills. It is not easy to always make my body cooperate with my mind. My mother worked with me every day until I grew confident on my stencils.

It was so hard to see things on the iPad keyboard. It hurt to look at the letters because I have strong eyes. My eyes see too much. It means I can see everything that makes up the letters like the minute details like the parts of the matter that make up the letters. Only I know how hard this is. I try to overcome the pain so I can spell. I think it helps to have different colors that are softer on the eyes. I have so much trouble with my motor skills. They make it hard to be still. To not have total control over your body is the worst obstacle ever. God is helping me get better at this.

I learned to point through practicing everyday with my mother. She taught me topics like science, math, Bible, geography, and read books to me. She would ask me choices about what we studied and I would select a choice. Then I would spell my answer on the stencils. This helped me make my finger listen to my mind more and more. My motor memory improved. Soon I was confident enough to spell in full sentences. Hope filled my heart.

My typing also got better. It still hurt to look at the keys but after a year I learned to focus—not my eyes, but my mind—on the letters inside my head. It is still hard to not type gibberish but with practice I am getting better. This is a goal so that people can see me type independently.

Then one day my mother read the Lord's Prayer and asked me what I prayed for. I spelled, "I H-A-V-E M-Y V-O-I-C-E." God answered my prayer then and there, and that was the day I got my voice. It was the best day of my life, I felt like my dreams came true, and I knew things would never be the same again.

Evolving Relationships with Others

My life changed forever that day because now I could say who saved me. Jesus saved me, and now I could tell the world. I could also tell my family I loved them. This made me so happy. My family was overjoyed they could talk to me after years of silence. They talked to me like they knew I was listening. This was not something they had done before. Now they knew I understood everything. They changed their expectations of me. I only had my expectations stay the same of them loving me the way I was. My family knew I was smart but now they treated me that way too.

Only my mother always spoke to me like I was an independent thinker. She always believed there was more inside me. But sometimes she still spoke to me in a condescending way. One time I advocated for myself by telling my mother not to speak to me like I was a baby. I told her that her speech belittled me when she said things in a simple manner like when she said "night-night" or "potty." She was so sorry. She promised to do better and sometimes she asks me how she's doing with talking to me.

I love having my family support me. They cheer me on all the time. Not so many people have such a loving family as mine. My sister Hope reads the books to me and Daddy helps me in gymnastics and my Mom teaches me every day. I am so happy they are mine and I am theirs.

Only my family knew I was intelligent, now others would know too. Everyone was so happy to hear from me and I was glad to share my really good voice with them.

Now my voice was being heard all over the world. My mother posted my words on my blog and so many people read them. My blog is called Rhemashope and it has thousands of followers. This might seem strange, but it made me feel shy to have my words read by so many. I am a very shy person, and I am often scared to share my thoughts with people I don't know. But I realized it was important for people to learn about autism from an autistic person. So I embraced the challenge, and I am glad I did.

My blog followers love to encourage me. I am so thankful for them because they believe in me. They make me want to succeed. I feel brave and truly strong because of their support. I am so happy I can share my thoughts with the world. This is my favorite thing to do. My only way to really have my voice heard besides at home. Can you imagine being silent for so long and then getting to speak to thousands? It is awesome.

Another gift was the gift of friendship. I began writing to a friend in Australia. She is autistic like me and we connect on such a deep level. Now I have a best friend named Sydney. She is a dream come true. I met her after going to a science class. She lives in my town. We started writing letters and having play dates. She really likes me and that makes me so happy. I always prayed for friends.

Only my relationships with the people who really believed in me changed. They started having conversations with me and expected to receive a response. It has been so nice to talk to people for the first time. Every time I talk to someone I get better at overcoming my nervousness. This is a goal of mine to talk to everyone I meet without being nervous. To talk to people is something I will never take for granted. To talk is a gift to one and all.

So talk to us (autistic people) like normal so we feel important. We may not respond with our timely voices but still know that we hear you and think you are lovely to speak to us. So much of talking happens inside with autistic people so we don't try to engage like others. But we want to so much. So try to remember this too. Strong to make others stomach the uncomfortable but we are thankful when you do your best.

So much of my world opened up when I found my voice. I mean that I found my way of communicating my story.

Schooling Experiences

One day I had to take a test that measures your intelligence. I had to take the test in order to show that I really could understand the age level subjects like science and history and math. I was so nervous because I knew how important this was. My parents had arranged for me to take the test over three days. I got better each time I went. They asked me questions on vocabulary words and math patterns and problems. The doctors were so nice and my friend Miss Jess was there to encourage me. Luckily I did well and was allowed to use my letter board. The doctor thought I was smart and should have a more challenging education.

I learn best when I am given challenging subjects to study. Nothing makes me happier than to study strong subjects. A strong subject is one you learn in school or at home where it is not simplified just because you cannot speak with your mouth. Strong subjects make me understand that learning can be fun. To study with my mother is one of my favorite things to do because she wants to show me new things so I can try to make my life better. We read books and study math and science and history and geography. I did not like it at first because I thought I would fail. I resisted studying with my mother at first because I did not believe I could do it. I was sure I would mess up and she would forget I was smart. God told me not to give up and to be brave. I think he told my mom the same thing. So he helped us both very much. I got better every day.

Only try to believe in your children no matter what they say because they are not always right. By "they" I mean the experts who don't really know everything about autism. No one thought I understood anything but now my voice is heard by thousands of people.

I have experienced inclusion in education. It was when my parents arranged for me to go to science class at my sister's school. This was so exciting because I love science and I decided that I wanted to become a scientist then and there. One day I took a science test and I did really well. My teacher said I was smart and that was the first time someone said that and really meant it, besides my parents.

Going to science class once a week was like having a taste of ice cream and having it fall off the cone. I wanted more. So my parents arranged for me to go more often but I had trouble staying in my seat. This was so sad and I did not get to go more than once a week. One day I got to participate in class when we played a game. I was so happy to be included. It was good to be on the same team as my best friend Syd. I did not talk but I was included.

Someone said that the only way to teach kids like me is to repeat things over and over, but that just frustrates us. We got it the first time, even though we can't always show you. To teach strong subjects should be the rule not the exception. How else can we learn if not given the chance to explore new ideas?

Some people do not believe it is me writing my words. One time a doctor came to my house and saw me point on my board. He did not believe I really could be a thinking human being. This made me so disappointed but this is the burden of my autism to constantly prove I am human too.

Many schools do not support the way I learned to type and point on my board. I think it truly is ridiculous. I can speak. It does not make a difference how I learned. The evidence is I once could not speak, now I can. It never makes sense to continue doing something that does not work. It only makes you insane. I am too young to be going insane. You speak, so you don't have a reason to change your methods. But stand a moment in my shoes and you will understand that having a voice is a gift so precious. The way you got it means nothing and yet it means everything. I hope teachers remember this so that people after me will have an easier time.

How can someone who doesn't believe ever believe in me? I should not have to make them believe. Love is always believing. Believing only takes someone who trusts that there is more than what they see. You don't forget that no matter how someone looks or acts they are worth believing in.

One time my old teacher visited me at my house and watched me type and do a poetry lesson. She told me she was sorry if she ever talked to me like I was not capable of understanding. This was so important to hear for me. It was better than anything else she could have said because she always believed in my abilities and now I could talk to her and say thank you.

I have been advocating for myself all my life. Like when I had to take that test so I could go to another school. To not advocate for myself would not be me. I hope it helps me get the education I so desperately want.

Not having a strong education is the saddest part of my life right now. I hope to go to a school where I can be challenged and have friends who see the real me. I should have access to the same education as anyone else. I hope to be a scientist one day. I hope to go to high school and college one day, too. So many possibilities are open to me now that I have my voice. I know I need lots of support, but I believe it is worth it. Someone once said the best students are the ones who really want to be there. That's me. So I will never stop trying to get the best education I can. I owe it to me and my family and other autistic people who have yet to find their voices.

To be able to get a challenging education for me is something for which my parents have been fighting for a long time. So many meetings and time and money spent just so I can have access to rigorous schooling. Time will tell how much their efforts mean to me.

As of September 2017, I am going to a new school! In my application to my new school I wrote:

> I learn best when I am given challenging subjects to study. This motivates me to do my best. For so long I have been taught to learn things in a repetitive nature. To have the same things taught over and over is truly making me insane. I love to learn new things and get a chance to explore new ideas. This makes me try to stay in my seat even when my body wants so much to get up and steal markers. I need lots of support to stay focused. To need this much help is a burden I am sorry to inflict on others but I do believe it is worth it. Only a few people have believed in me. I hope you will too.
>
> I communicate by pointing on my board and typing. This is a slow way but it is the only way until I can talk with my mouth. Soon I will be able to talk with my own voice through my iPad. This makes me so happy. Not having a speaking voice is so hard. I hope you will understand that I want to talk to you and think you are lovely to speak to me.
>
> I want you to know that I am autistic and that is something I am happy and sad about. I love that God made me this way even though it is so hard sometimes. I can hear music in trees and grass and numbers have sounds that make me so joyous. I also can remember just about everything I hear. The reason I said it makes me sad is because I can't talk with my mouth and that is so hard to not have the ability to just speak whenever. I know it seems like I am not smart but I am. I believe one day I will show the world that autistic people are smart and want the same things as anyone else. Thank you for being patient with me while I learn to sit in class. I want to have an education that helps me reach my goals.
>
> I do not have a least favorite subject. I am happy just to get challenging subjects at all. The end.

I love my new school. The teachers really believe in my intelligence. I go to science and math classes with my mother as my aide. My good mother works with me every day to complete my homework. I am so excited to be in a class of students that are at my grade level. I cannot wait to learn all there is to learn.

My hope is to stay in my seat and not grab markers. I am getting better at sitting in class and having control over my impulses. My ability to be in more classes depends on how much I can improve my stamina in school.

I have a new friend named Reilly. She loves people with her heart. She is full of good ideas. She talks to me even though I can't talk back. She sees me past my embarrassing moments. She writes long letters and encourages. She is a true friend. Having a friend in school is a dream come true.

I answer questions on my iPad. I am slow to type but my teachers are patient and so are my classmates. Mrs. Corbin calls on me in class. She sends me messages of encouragement. Mrs. Baker came to my house to watch me do math. She is the nicest teacher I have ever had.

This is what I have been waiting for all my life. I am forging a new path so I can follow my dreams. Someone once said just because you have a disability doesn't mean you can't have dreams. We all have dreams. I am on my way. Finally.

Recommendations to Support Students Like Me

The kind of communication partner I need is one who is patient and believes in my abilities and is willing to practice with me. She helps me focus my mind on what I am doing. I get distracted so easily by everything around me and my noise in my head gets so loud. The communication partner really helps me to listen to the right sounds in my head. This takes lots of practice and trust. I hope to be able to do this more and more so I can be a better communicator.

Having a communication partner hold the iPad or board helps me focus my too stimulated mind. To have the iPad on the table with no one holding it is a goal for me. I am getting so much better at that. I hope to be completely independent on my iPad one day. By that I mean that I won't need a partner to hold the iPad while I type.

How do you include people who type or point? You treat them just like you would treat any student. Give them an opportunity to learn and share their thoughts. I think the way to do this is to let students pick their schools so they can be a part of the process.

One time I gave a speech to a class of future teachers. This is what I said:

> We choose to make decisions on how to teach students by strong belief in their potential. Notice only that they really want to succeed like everyone else.
>
> Teachers should really try to show their students that they are happy to teach them really strong subjects.
>
> I hope the teachers try to help their students feel like they might succeed. How else can they succeed?
>
> If they do not have strong attention spans they will need to have someone help them stay on task. I hate to need this, but I do so much love to learn so I am thankful to go to school.
>
> Nothing helps me more than having people who try to believe in me. If they do not, I will know it, and I will fail. That is why I am thankful for Soma and my mother. Thousands of people now hear my words because my mother did not give up.
>
> I think that teachers should try to make students do meaningful work so that they have something interesting to study. Nothing makes me so frustrated as having the same thing taught over and over. It makes me so mad I cannot try to do better and I very much hate that I do not have better subjects. I mean science, math, history, reading good stories in school.
>
> I had a good teacher who taught me to spell on a letter board. She believed in me when no one else did. She taught me to believe in myself when I had given up hope. Her name is Soma and I will always be grateful to her for helping me. Time will tell how much she changed my life. Thank God for Soma.
>
> My strong desire is to have a challenging education. I want to be a scientist. Not something I would have thought so much possible years ago but now I think it is possible.
>
> Strong minds should have strong education. Not strong minds should have strong educations too. Good education is a goal for me.
>
> Thank you for inviting me to your class. Only try to be patient with your students. They need your support so much. They will do well to study important things.

Nothing makes me happier than to share my story. My hope is that this has been helpful. Thank you for listening to me.

Before I could use my board and type I could not tell people how I felt, what I understood, or if I was hurting. They often treated me like I was a baby. This was so frustrating to me but I hoped one day they would know the real me. Someone once said I was stupid because I could not talk. This hurt so much. Only now can I look back and see that it made me stronger. Now I have my voice and lots of people read my words. This makes me so happy. The silence is over. The pain is gone. And I am free.

> you might wonder how i can talk
> in my head
> but not
> in my mouth
> like the most glorious morning
> my words rise in my mind
> i want to shout them to the world
> like rivers they flow on
> my words
> then they pool
> at the bottom of the waterfall
> they have no way out
> my mouth inhibits their passage
> only the river knows them
> only those who tread the waters
> can ever hear

Love, Rhema

Conclusion:
Research-Based Recommendations for Educators and Therapists

EDLYN VALLEJO PEÑA, PH.D.

The collective voices represented in this book illuminate the tumultuous and awe-inspiring journeys autistics who use letter boards and keyboards endured to access communication and inclusion in schools and communities. The stories narrated by Tracy, Larry, and Amy—all of whom grew up in a time when institutionalization was common— underscore the idea that it is never too late to introduce an individual to meaningful communication. When communication choice, access, and supports were granted to Tracy, Larry, and Amy, new windows of opportunities opened in their lives. The younger generation of authors highlight the delicate process of navigating the current political climate of accessing communication and educational inclusion in school systems. In one way or another, all of them fought against schools that were unwilling or unequipped to educate them. While Ido, Samuel, Dillan, Henry, Emma, Philip, and Rhema encountered challenges with school systems, their early access to communication, compared to that of Tracy, Larry, and Amy, suggests a shift in awareness and attitudes about RPM and FC. All ten authors' resilience and self-advocacy have paved a path of opportunity for the younger generation of autistic students who will one day require augmentative and alternative communication supports. Barriers are breaking. When structural limitations are eliminated, buoyed by proper resources and attitudes in schools and communities, an autistic child or adult can achieve what was once considered impossible.

In recent years, research about practices that support students who use letter boards and keyboards to communicate in educational settings have emerged. Articles by Ashby & Kasa (2013), Woodfield and Ashby (2016), and Ashby, Woodfield, and Delia (2016) provide excellent recommendations for educators and therapists seeking information on supporting the inclusion and communication needs of minimally speaking and nonspeaking students. To build on to the existing research, this concluding chapter weaves together the most common recommendations made by the ten chapter authors along with original research results from a study I conducted on promising practices to support students who type and spell to communicate. The results of the research study are based on interviews of 14 school and college educators. All of them played a role in teams that supported the education of students who type or spell to communicate using letter boards, keyboards, and tablets. The participants included school teachers, communication partners, behavioral therapists, speech language pathologists, university faculty, and university disability resource center staff. The educators and therapists I interviewed were nominated by autistic individuals and service providers for being exemplary in their advocacy and dedication to students who type and spell to communicate. The 14 individuals, hailing from both public and private schools and colleges, reflect a small sample of the dozens of educators and professionals across the United States who currently teach, advise, and support students who type or spell to communicate. To keep participants' interview responses confidential, pseudonyms are used for participants' names. In total, 10 autistic authors and 14 educators and therapists informed the research findings presented in this chapter.

The research-based recommendations are organized into a framework of three dimensions of support which educators and therapists can provide to nonspeaking autistic students. First, they must be willing to be vulnerable and courageous in admitting they were wrong in their preconceived notions about students with autism. Their working paradigms about nonspeaking autistic students require a shift from deficit-based notions about students to presuming competence in students (Biklen & Burke, 2006). In addition, supportive individuals are willing to become institutional agents—"those individuals who have the capacity and commitment to transmit directly, or negotiate the transmission of, institutional resources and opportunities" (Stanton-Salazar, 1997, p. 6) to students. Second, educators and therapists must provide access to communication, including communication tools, a trained communication partner, and sensory and motor supports. Third, educators and therapists must construct opportunities for student participation and engagement. Doing so involves educating students in the context of age-appropriate instruction and inclusive environments, arranging opportunities for students to actively participate in learning environments, and creating opportunities for the student to develop self-advocacy skills. These three dimensions of support are vital to educating and empowering minimally speaking and nonspeaking students. Figure 1 visually depicts the framework.

FIGURE 1: FRAMEWORK TO SUPPORT STUDENTS
WHO TYPE AND SPELL TO COMMUNICATE

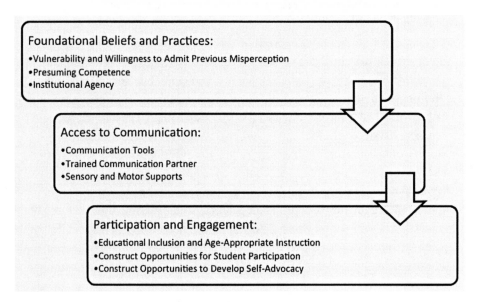

Foundational Beliefs and Practices:
• Vulnerability and Willingness to Admit Previous Misperception
• Presuming Competence
• Institutional Agency

Access to Communication:
• Communication Tools
• Trained Communication Partner
• Sensory and Motor Supports

Participation and Engagement:
• Educational Inclusion and Age-Appropriate Instruction
• Construct Opportunities for Student Participation
• Construct Opportunities to Develop Self-Advocacy

Foundational Beliefs

The approaches and practices of supportive educators and therapists are grounded in a system of beliefs and practices. These beliefs and practices establish a foundation for the opportunities and accommodations provided to minimally speaking and nonspeaking autistic students.

Vulnerability and Willingness
to Admit Previous Misperceptions

First, educators and therapists who are successful in supporting students who type and spell to communicate engage in acts of vulnerability by admitting that their preconceived notions about autistic students and how to educate them were wrong. In his chapter, Dillan explained both the complexities and significance of this experience:

> The people in charge of making policy in education often believe they already have all the answers, and their rigid thinking makes it difficult for them to accept that they may be wrong or have incomplete information. A person must be willing to question themselves and the entire weight of a system of education built around false premises that students like me are hopelessly simple-minded. That is not only difficult to do, but dangerous to your career because the education system is rigid and hostile to rogue elements that seek to do things differently.

The chapter authors acknowledge they were provided opportunities once educators and therapists were willing to question their own assumptions when presented with information that stood in contradiction to their understanding of autistic students. In contrast, when educators and therapist were, as Ido described, "resistant to new ideas, resistant to change, and rigid and concrete in visualizing the possibility of their students having greater potential," students stood little chance of being granted the chance to communicate using their preferred mode of communication. Educators and therapists, Emma argues, must challenge their deeply rooted ideas "that autism does not automatically mean—can't, won't, or doesn't." Further, Ido maintains, "Being open-minded and admitting that the brain is vast and mysterious is required, in my opinion, by anyone who works with severely autistic people."

Many of the educators and therapists in the study described their "ah-ha" moment of realizing they were wrong about minimally speaking and nonspeaking students with autism. Table 1 presents examples of the moments in which they questioned and were forced to "unlearn" their assumptions about students with minimal to no speech.

TABLE 1: EXAMPLES OF VULNERABILITY
AND WILLINGNESS TO ADMIT PREVIOUS MISPERCEPTION

Participant	*Quote*
Desiree (behavioral supervisor and communication partner)	"I got to shadow this person who had already been supporting this girl in middle school. She was typing with her and everything. I remember just at first not really believing it. It was weird. It's like my eyes knew what they were seeing but my head couldn't quite wrap my brain.... I couldn't wrap my brain around it, right? Because it was so disjointed. It was mismatched. The way she presented which we know now, the presentation is so different from what was coming out of the Dynavox. It was a Dynavox machine at the time."
Drake (behavior interventionist and communication partner)	"You have to unlearn how you're used to dealing with people in general and how you're taught to think of dealing with people.... I realized really quick I just had to drop everything I'd been taught up to that point because it wasn't working. That model wasn't working."
Grace (paraeducator and communication partner)	"We have now recognized that we are maybe doing something wrong, or that maybe there's another way to do it, or that you can still grow. Maybe that's not the right way. Maybe some people who are a skeptic of RPM think that that's not an effective method, but something still needs to change. You have to keep all of these doors open so that we can grow, and we can problem solve, and we can figure out how to best support our students. If somebody is closed-minded to one method, then that takes away from that growth, and that takes away from basically human rights. This is a civil rights thing."
Sharon (head of school for students with developmental disabilities and sensory-movement differences)	"I wish that we had listened to the autistic and disability community from day one. Instead of being guided by professionals.... We made some big mistakes and I'm very open and vulnerable about talking about them."
Alexis (paraeducator and communication partner)	"I watched a video of [the student doing RPM]... I started crying. It was just intense. It was really intense. Feeling like, at that point I guess I was with him maybe five years, but I felt like family, and you've been working with this person for so long and all the sudden their world has changed and your world has changed and it opens up this whole new life and so I was amazed by it."

Presuming Competence

After individuals take a critical look at their assumptions, they can move toward presuming competence in autistic students. In her chapter, Emma explained that presuming competence involves a presumption "that each and every student, whether they can speak or not, can and will eventually learn given the necessary supports and encouragement." In Dillan's words, it means "believing that they [nonspeaking autistic students] are capable of understanding, thinking about, and processing the knowledge of the world around them." The importance of presuming competence has been emphasized by many advocates, practitioners, and researchers (e.g., Biklen & Burke, 2006). Even though this is not a new concept, the presumption of competence is a central belief necessary to supporting students who type and spell to communication. This is because—as Arne Duncan, the former United States Secretary of Education, argued—"No belief is more damaging in education than the misperception that children with disabilities cannot really succeed and shouldn't be challenged to reach the same high standards as all children" (2010, para. 4). All of the chapter authors, at some point, describe the detrimental results of being "limited by low expectations," as Ido puts it. Amy, for instance, "had to go through years of non-learning, because of the presumption of incompetence." That was until she "was lucky enough to meet people who simply assumed I could absorb information and have thoughts." Tracy argues, "It is imperative that educators think about presuming competence and look for ways to see the intelligence in all of us." After all, Dillan notes, "No progress will ever be made in a classroom where each adult sees only empty heads and broken minds in their students." Table 2 presents examples of ways in which educators and therapists expressed the importance of presuming competence in their students.

TABLE 2: EXAMPLES OF THE IMPORTANCE OF PRESUMING COMPETENCE

Participant	Quote
Sharon (head of school for students with developmental disabilities and sensory-movement differences)	"They [educators] cannot believe that these kids have the intellectual capacity that they do. That's what I feel like is the biggest block, I don't think it's so much the [letter] boards or the FC, I think people have a block with believing in their cognitive levels."

Participant	*Quote*
Ariana (district inclusion facilitator and special education teacher)	"That's where the districts and the teachers have to start ... believing that these kids are capable if given the right resources, the right opportunities, and I think they have to be treated respectfully. You have to treat students that may not look like they know anything or may not look like they understand, we have to treat them as if they do and then teach them as if they do. Because if we don't we lose their respect and so we don't have these kids by the time they get to middle school with extremely challenging behaviors."
Kristy (assistant teacher)	"The main thing is presuming competence. That is my number one [recommendation]. If you presume competence and teach age level appropriate material and talk to them just like you would anyone else their age and show them that respect, I mean, you can't go wrong."
Tiffany (university disability resource center coordinator)	"[The student] told me that really hit home was that he really appreciated me not treating him any differently than the other students. He just wanted to be treated like a college student. From day one, I just talked to him like I'd talk to all the other students because I didn't know any different. I figured, here's a young man who, he's here, he's in college, and so I'm going to treat him and talk to him like a college student. I think that that's maybe the first bit of advice, is just to talk to them like you would any other student."

Institutional Agency

Another important factor in supporting students who use letter boards and keyboards to communicate is institutional agency. Institutional agents are people who can help students navigate the educational culture, resources, and politics to be successful. These individuals are typically well positioned to provide key forms of social and institutional support. They use their agency to advocate for students, particularly those who are members of historically under-served groups. The chapter authors acknowledge that while their efforts, persistence, and resilience are paramount to their own success, they cannot thrive without key institutional agents in their lives to support them. As an example, to gain access to college, Samuel explains that, "a strong, motivated, equipped transition team, and significant professional collaboration is a big part of the solution for autistic students hopeful to attend college and other postsecondary programs." The quotes in Table 3 reflect various ways educators and therapists have had to navigate, advocate, and assert their agency for students who communicate in diverse ways. Some of these strategies were overt, some were covert, but all were pivotal to students' circumnavigating systemic barriers.

TABLE 3: EXAMPLES OF INSTITUTIONAL AGENCY

Participant	Quote
Desiree (behavioral supervisor and communication partner)	"When I first met [my student], he was in a self-contained autism class. It was crazy. I walked in there and … it felt like a hospital…. I remember people telling me about [my student], about him in front of him. It was really hard. I remember them telling me, 'Okay. He's going to do this to you. He's going to run away'… It was terrible. I remember having to be really careful. I wasn't going to come in there. I couldn't just step on people's toes. I had to work within this classroom in the beginning…. We kind of did things on the down low and then we were able to convince them that when we looked behaviorally enough in control to try mainstreaming, you know?"
Drake (behavior interventionist and communication partner)	"I usually kind of pull in my team. I have a really good supervisor who I really trust her opinion on. Anytime I've felt bad we've kind of discussed what our options are…. I think she actually at one point had a handout almost to give to all of his teachers saying this is to make you aware that [the student] is going in your classroom and that here are some of his specific needs and here's kind of what it looks like and that he may do sort of silly behavior but don't give into that and don't give him that negative attention. [The handout is] kind of a primer on dealing with him."
Leanne (resource teacher)	"I have been advocating that we need to find [a more accepting] school psychologist in the county who is open to this [kind of communication], and will test my students [with the accommodation of a letter board or keyboard]. I've asked my department head to speak to [the current school psychologist] before meetings with parents to ask her to just make sure she's being polite at least. I think everyone knows how she feels, that she should be respectful to those parents. In general I honestly

Participant	Quote
	don't have much to do with her, I reassure my students that I know they're smart, and it doesn't matter what a psychologist who's never met them thinks. I've had to calm parents down too, because they've gotten that understanding from her."
Ariana (district inclusion facilitator and special education teacher)	"Here's this kid with pretty challenging behaviors and extremely.... Some people would just say autistic. Non-verbal, clapping, noisy, and kind of a behaviorally challenging kid that most teachers would say he doesn't belong in general ed.... I had to fight to support him by a lot of talking with my department in terms of the support that he needed and why somebody else couldn't do it. They agreed, but they also said that this is an exception."
Tiffany (university disability resource center coordinator)	"I developed [a student profile] document and some things to share with faculty.... The document said, what kind of furniture is needed, and considering that there's going to be communication partner present, so as a dynamic it's good to be seated next to one another, side by side, front to back. Even those types of things that would be important to share with the faculty who's going to be teaching the specific course. The document also talks about the student's learning style. What is the best way that a student learned, you know, auditory, does the student have a need to record lectures, because that would be something to consult with the faculty member to let them know. And then participation in class, so it's important to know how would the student communicate in class when they have a question and what that looks like with the communication partner present. How do they determine and how do they express that if the student has a question, the student raised his hand, [or] if the communication partner raised their hand?"

Access to Communication

Once educators and therapists established the beliefs and skills necessary to support autistic students, they became better equipped to support the student's preferred mode of communication. Chapter authors and the study's participants named three critical elements to access communication: the communication tools themselves, trained communication partners, and sensory and motor supports.

Communication Tools

It goes without saying that the first requirement in gaining tangible access to communication is the provision of communication tools themselves. Letter boards, keyboard, white boards and dry erase markers, tablets with communication apps, and other tools are used among individuals who type and spell to communicate. Some use one communication tool at a time and others use a multi-modal approach to communicate depending on the situation and context. Larry described his mode of communication as, "fickle technology dependent, potentially printed out, typing." Access to typing translates to exchanges of ideas and participation in opportunities. For Larry, access to typing is his gateway to "self-actualization."

A report by the U.S. Department of Education (2016) explains "auxiliary aids and services that help to ensure effective communication for students with disabilities" can include "word or letter boards" and "spelling to communicate" (p. 43). A list of approved communication-related accommodations that have been documented in the IEPs of students who type and spell to communicate across the United States is included as an appendix to this book. Educators and therapists must advocate for schools to include such auxiliary aids and services as a documented accommodation in students' individualized education plans (IEPs). The U.S. Department of Education report makes clear that "school districts must therefore ensure that they comply with both the IDEA and the effective communication requirements under Title II for students with disabilities" (p. 43). Otherwise, students pay a steep educational price. Ido explains the potential consequences to being denied access to communication tools:

> My one finger typing or pointing to letters has been the difference between stagnation in a low remedial autism program and receiving a general education. It is the difference between being thought to be a concrete thinker and being known to be funny, compassionate and intelligent. My one finger typing is the equivalent of sign language to a deaf person. It is my modality of communication and it gives me access to the world and control over my life.

Trained Communication Partner

Chapter authors as well as the educators and therapists in the study could not overstate the importance of having access to a trained communication partner. Given the complexities involved in supporting individual student's dynamic communication needs, along with accommodating their motor and sensory differences, an untrained communication partner cannot suffice. Communication partners must undergo extensive training from an experienced professional who can coach them on various facets of supporting communication needs in school settings. The communication partner must spend time practicing communication with the student to build rapport before expecting reliable communication. Open-ended, fluid communication does not happen overnight. Communication partners and communicators must spend weeks, and even months, getting in sync with each other. Without proper training and rapport building, communication partners are unhelpful to the student, at best, and damaging to the student's academic and psychological well-being, at worst. Tracy explains, "Communication has been a big-time complicated journey that involves finding capable support staff to learn about my communication." Organizations such as the Institute on Communication and Inclusion at Syracuse University, Helping Autism through Learning and Outreach (HALO), and other organizations that offer augmentative and alternative communication supports can be consulted for specific information about training and professional development standards.

Professional development aimed toward training communication partners must not ignore the academic and emotional support needs of autistic students. Ido, for instance, expects to work with a communication partner who is able to multi-task and navigate the accommodations necessary for him to participate moment-to-moment in class. He has had success with communication partners "who could easily follow my communication pointing to letters, had the ability to support me in class in terms of my restlessness, as well as serve as a scribe by writing down my in-class essays or in filling in the bubbles on tests for me." In addition, communication partners must support the student in social and emotional ways. Rhema underscores the kind of social and emotional support she expects from a communication partner: "The kind of communication partner I need is one who is patient and believes in my abilities and is willing to practice with me. She helps me focus my mind on what I am doing." Table 4 presents examples of various ways properly trained communication partners are necessary to student success. The large number of quotes in the table demonstrates the wide range of skills required to provide dynamic communicative, academic, and emotional support, often by multiple communication partners.

TABLE 4: EXAMPLES OF THE IMPORTANCE OF TRAINED COMMUNICATION PARTNERS

Participant	Quote
Kristy (assistant teacher)	"[I recommend] definitely having trained staff because a lot of people think they can just pick up a board and if the kid knows RPM, then it's magically going to happen, which isn't the case. You have to be skilled, you have to know what you're doing which requires a lot of work. I believe if a child is RPMing in a school, they need to be with someone who is highly skilled in RPM."
Alexis (paraeducator and communication partner)	"You can't start a facilitator and a student on the first day of school say, 'Here you go. Go to class. Have fun. Good luck.' Knowing that there's going to have to be some training and some hours outside of school. There needs to be some sort of consultant to train them. There should be periodic training, as well."
Leanne (resource teacher)	"I support these students academically, but it's so much more than just having an RPM lesson, it's beyond the framework of that, because they're using these tools, whether it's typing on a letter board, or on a wireless keyboard, or directly into their iPad. They're using that to access curriculum and communication with classmates, communicate with teachers."
Ariana (district inclusion facilitator and special education teacher)	"That support person is a critical piece, I've learned. I continue to learn how critical that piece is, and how it's an emotional connection. You can't.... Most of these kids have a very difficult time just typing with anybody. Once they start typing with somebody then another person comes and sits down next to them so they continue with their typing. There seems to have to be a connection."
Tiffany (university disability resource center coordinator)	"He also had access to a communication partner in his [university] entry assessments to place him in English and Math courses."
Desiree (behavioral supervisor and communication partner)	"If you had a school onboard ... [they provide] a trained support partner going six hours a day with that student and having multiple opportunities

Participant	*Quote*
	throughout the day to practice… [Without a trained communication partner] they can't demonstrate what they really know and so then guess what? Where are they going to end up? They're going to end up in an autism classroom, and they're not going to be learning age appropriate materials that are meaningful for them. Right? They won't be seen or heard or understood. That's why I say that's a death sentence."
Rianna (university communication partner)	"Using the keyboard, she's a lot faster, and requires less support. At home we'll use that one. It's just something really short, or if she's having an emotional time, and just needs to get something out fast, we'll use her keyboard instead of her letter board. If it's homework or something that requires someone else to read it, we do it on the iPad. On the iPad, there's a lot more support that's required by way of touching at her elbow. Depending on her mood, how she's feeling, I'll read what she's writing just to keep her on track with her thought, whereas with the keyboard…. Like her shoulder, or lightly touch her upper arm."
Grace (paraeducator and communication partner)	"He is able, he's at a point with his speech pathologist where he needs no prompts, no pencil, no verbal prompts, no physical prompts other than her holding the board in front of him. We're still getting to a point where we can put it on the table. He can do, like I said, he can write paragraphs for her, and she only has to hold the board. She doesn't have to say a word or do anything with her hands. Then he gets on the board with me or his other provider. I have to use verbal prompts, not physical, but verbal. With another provider, he's only at the stencil board using a pencil. There's three different providers that he has to use the letter board in three different ways. People don't understand that."
Drake (behavior interventionist and communication partner)	"A lot of times I advocate for him to get out his iPad, say hi to people when they say hi to him and talk to them, have a conversation and mediate that so that he gets that social interaction because that's definitely something he wants to have from people is he wants to have friends and he wants to have meaningful conversations with people but he doesn't really always know how to initiate them so sometimes I have given him a little push to remind him to engage in a conversation [with somebody]."

Support Sensory and Motor Differences

The majority of authors in the book spoke of the challenges that plagued them with their motor and sensory systems (Donnellan, Hill, & Leary, 2013). Tracy pointedly notes, "My greatest deficit has always been motor." Add sensory dysregulation to that, and the experience can be unbearable. Tracy explains, "Going up the ladder of anxiety is a familiar course for me when I am on sensory overload and with lack of intentional movement I get stressed as well, making it hard to think and communicate what is going on in my mind." A number of the authors acknowledged the difficulty in coordinating movements to simply point to one letter at a time. Rhema beautifully explains what her mind and body go through when she practices pointing to letters: "To communicate this way I had to learn how to make my finger point to the letters inside my head. This is harder than it sounds because I have so much trouble with my motor skills. It is not easy to always make my body cooperate with my mind." The "mind-body disconnect," Ido clarifies, is the reason why autistic individuals have a difficult time using both hands simultaneously to spell and type messages. In his chapter, Samuel echoes similar experiences with coordinating his typing: "It is difficult to get my mind and body on the same page, so using one finger to spell decreases the demand for motor planning and coordination." This concept is rarely understood. According to Dillan, educators and therapists "do not realize that I do not have the intentional control to get my hand where I wanted it to go." Table 5 presents examples of ways in which educators and therapists in the study took into consideration sensory and motor differences among their students.

TABLE 5: EXAMPLES OF TAKING INTO ACCOUNT SENSORY
AND MOTOR DIFFERENCES

Participant	Quote
Grace (paraeducator and communication partner)	"Autism is a motor processing disorder.... The disability is also in initiation. That's why it's hard. It's not necessarily that he doesn't comprehend. It's that his body is not listening to the signals that his mind is firing. I'm constantly having to explain those kind of things. I think that people understand it, but I think that also it's been said for so long that our kids don't comprehend, they're not intelligent, they're not empathetic, they're not all these differ-

Participant	Quote
	ent things. To have somebody come in who is younger and say, 'Actually I think that he's got all of those things, it's just his body's not listening to him.' I think that's hard for some people to take in."
Ariana (district inclusion facilitator and special education teacher)	"I know that a lot of it too is teaching kids how to regulate their bodies, and so I think that's a big part of it too. Can they start out in school sitting all day long, looking like everyone else, perfectly able to control their bodies? No. We have to give them opportunities in teaching, teach them from the early stages how to regulate themselves. That's how [the student] is getting to be so successful. He's really worked really hard on that piece. Sometimes I forget, I just want to sit down with a kid and, 'Come on, let's get to work.' They're all dis-regulated. 'Come on, type! Type, kid, type!' Stick the keyboard in front of them or whatever when [instead] we need to maybe do some breathing or go for a walk or talk about, maybe we just need to talk about feelings first. Get regulated, get the body regulated. Again, it's just so individual, what a kid needs."
Alexis (paraeducator and communication partner)	"I'm still, though, holding the Bluetooth [keyboard] and just giving some verbal coaching and some verbal support as he is typing. When he's upset or he's body's more disorganized, I may jump in and give him more verbal support or gestural [prompts]"
Kristy (assistant teacher)	"I was working with a student that if you put either a paintbrush or a marker or anything in her hand, she'll just start scribbling automatically. What I did was I wanted to slow down that automatic process and I used the board to have her explain to me what she wanted her picture to look like, what color she wanted, how many flowers she wanted, all these things. Then she would point on the canvas where she wanted to place each thing. Then, when she had the paintbrush her movements were intentional and she could do what it was that she was pictured. I've never seen her so proud of herself."
Sharon (head of school for students with developmental disabilities and sensory-movement differences)	"That's going to instill change, if I can get some principals, the administration, to buy into the brain/body disconnect then I think everything else will be gravy."

Participation and Engagement

The last dimension to the framework of supporting students who use letter boards and keyboards to communicate involves constructing opportunities for inclusion and meaningful learning, active participation, and self-advocacy.

Educational Inclusion and Age-Appropriate Instruction

The authors argue for meaningful inclusion in an age-appropriate curriculum and social opportunities with typical peers. Tracy's argument for inclusion is compelling: "Inclusion, like communication, is paramount to healthy children and long term success. I want educators to understand that all children benefit from inclusion because all children can make contributions with proper supports." All chapter authors experienced segregation and exclusion to some degree, a sign of continued injustices against autistic students. In his chapter, Larry, a product of extreme exclusion and institutionalization, reflects on the educational and social opportunities on which he missed out. Larry emphasizes the need to interact with neurotypical peers inside and outside of school because,

> You will have to learn life in the community early on. Play on the same playgrounds as other kids and look ahead to college and a career. Participating in everyday activities with peers teaches you social interaction.... Practicing patterns of social interactions regularly with your iPad that will propel your voices into the bright future.

Philip, who gained entrée into an inclusive general education classroom by the time he reached 7th grade, marvels at the opportunities inclusion provided him to develop social relationships with typical peers. He described what it was like for him "making friends in regular classes." He admitted that,

> learning to interact socially is still a big challenge, but I have been able to make friends in my own way. My friends give me questions on index cards and I answer them on my own time. It has been nice to be noticed and included. People think I am interesting. I am not what they expected. I like that my classmates talk normally to me. They try to include me as an equal.

The learning that happens inside classrooms with meaningful and engaging instruction also paves the way for students' academic success.

As Henry notes, "All students should be taught how to read and have curriculum that is age appropriate. Teaching the same simple thing year after year does not help anyone." Rhema's recommendation is that,

> teachers should try to make students do meaningful work so that they have something interesting to study. Nothing makes me so frustrated as having the same thing taught over and over. It makes me so mad I cannot try to do better and I very much hate that I do not have better subjects. I mean science, math, history, reading good stories in school.

One must not forget that this kind of access to the curriculum requires access to appropriate accommodations. In addition to communication tools, other kinds of accommodations must be in place to level the playing field for autistic students in the classroom. Samuel describes what is required of successful inclusion in his college classes: "I receive extended time for exams, a quiet room if necessary, a note-taker, audio-versions of my textbooks, priority registration, access to my communication partner, access to my assistive technology (AT), and I meet with my professors in advance." Table 6 offers examples of ways in which educators and therapists make sense of the benefits of inclusion and age-appropriate instruction.

TABLE 6: EXAMPLES OF HOW AND WHY INCLUSION WORKS

Participant	Quote
Declan (speech language pathologist)	"[We need to] be sensitive to sensory needs of these kids on the spectrum but we also need to be strong and provide them opportunities to learn their academic skills: reading, writing, and speaking, on par with a typically developing child. We know there is a delay in their motor skills, but we need to develop a curriculum where we work on holding a pencil, writing, we should introduce curriculum as you would in a general education. The earlier we start, the better they will be."
Kristy (assistant teacher)	"It's worth saying again in this context, if you presume competence and teach age level appropriate material and talk to them just like you would anyone else their age and show them that respect, you can't go wrong."
Drake (behavior interventionist and communication partner)	"Now that he has come a ways, he has little moments here and there where it's cool when he knows the answer to a question and types it, and types it before anybody else in the general ed class says it. Those are cool moments."

Participant	Quote
Steve (university professor)	"We were working on an assignment that essentially asks them to look critically at their eating habits. We were talking about vegetarianism and veganism and how culture influences what we eat. It's kind of an interesting thought exercise that a lot of them haven't really considered, and [the students] being kind of, I think he's gluten-free, I don't remember exactly what he said, but the conversation was not necessarily as stimulating as I was hoping it to be, and [this student] hopped in there and just had a really savvy response to the article we were reading, and basically he sort of modeled what I wanted them to do was to have a critical response to the article and then use a personal experience to tie in and have those things go back and forth. Once he did that, that really got the conversation going. I think everyone else jumped on that, and they're like, 'Oh, okay, this is what we're supposed to be doing.'"
Tiffany (university disability resource center coordinator)	"He has had the opportunity to be a speaker at several college events and I know recently, there's a [volunteer] club on campus … and they have an event and [the student] got to be part of that. I think it's just saying that the student is literally facing his path."

Construct Opportunities for Participation

Whether a student is included in general education or placed into a special education classroom, educators and communication partners must provide opportunities for the student to actively participate in developing knowledge, critical thinking skills, and meaningful experiences. Some of the authors experienced rich opportunities in which they were encouraged to engage and participate in instruction while others did not. In the absence of experiencing a rich education experience, Amy notes in her chapter, "What I am most proud of knowing, is the history and the continuing fight for disability rights. I know what I know because I have been reading what other disabled people write. I know what I know because I meet, in real life and online, other disabled people." Amy accessed learning through audio books, social media, the news, and poetry writing classes. Ideally, these opportunities should be offered to students by educators and therapists so that autistic students don't have to fight for them. Rhema contends that schools should "give [students] an opportunity to learn and share their thoughts." Encouraging participation in learning activities must involve students' accommodations. Henry applauded one of his teachers for honoring his accommodations to participate: "She let me point to the multiple-choice questions instead of circling them. She let me type the answers to the spelling tests instead of using a pencil. Miss R also let me be the line leader and be part of the class. I learned a lot and I made good grades." The examples that educators and therapists in the study shared, presented in Table 7, depict rich opportunities in which students with autism were provided a chance to participate and engage in learning environments in meaningful ways.

TABLE 7: CONSTRUCTING OPPORTUNITIES FOR PARTICIPATION

Participant	*Quote*
Drake (behavior interventionist and communication partner)	"The first time that [the student] ever used FC ... in front of a class was he did a presentation with a group on the Bahamas for this presentation for his geography class. He typed out his speech. When it came to be his turn he hit his speak button and it read his speech for him and that was the first time he'd ever done anything like that. He talked about it for a month afterwards, like, 'Wasn't that so cool that I got up and gave the speech.' That was really neat to see."
Grace (paraeducator and communication partner)	"When I was first starting at this school we were in an inclusion class and it was digital photography.... I said, 'Okay, clearly I know nothing about these subjects, so here's your chance to teach me. Will you please teach me about this? What elements of art and principles of design are in that picture?' He ended up spelling that the picture showed unity, and rhythm, and there was another one.... I said, 'Is it okay if I share this with the class?' He says, 'Yes.' I shared it with the teacher. I think unity was one where my student ... nobody else in the classroom had picked that word or put that principle. The teacher was just floored. He was like, 'Oh my gosh. That actually works. I see what you're talking about. You are absolutely correct. The colors in this are unified through blah, blah, blah.' Just having him take that out and having the teacher say ... and I got to learn. I think that showing him that he was teaching

Participant	Quote
	me, it was just a huge accomplishment and one of the best moments that I've had with RPM for sure."
Steve (university professor)	"[The student] from the get-go was always very participatory in the whole group discussions, so he would essentially, I could kind of see him pointing out a response to [his communication partner], out of the corner of my eye as I'm scanning the room looking for students to respond... [He] really established himself as one of the more consistent participants in the whole group discussions"
Rianna (university communication partner)	"Her English teacher really highlights spoken presentations, and that stresses her out quite a bit. It kind of puts her in a little mood, because she wants so badly to be a part of those assignments, but instead she has her iPad.... I'll have to talk with [the student] real quick. 'We're going to do it this way, and it'll all be great. The students are going to love it. Your presentation is going to be just as awesome.'"

Construct Opportunities to Develop Self-Advocacy

As evidenced in their chapter narratives, the authors developed strong self-advocacy skills to make a case for access to their communication, inclusion, and other resources to improve their quality of life. The Autistic Self Advocacy Network describes self-advocacy as part of the disability rights movement where,

> autistic people enjoy equal access, rights, and opportunities ... to take control of our own lives and the future of our common community, and seek to organize the autistic community to ensure our voices are heard in the national conversation about us. Nothing About Us, Without Us! [ASAN, n.d., para. 1].

While providing opportunities for autistic individuals to develop self-advocacy skills was only mentioned by a few educators and therapists in the study, this particular theme strongly emerged among the narratives of the autistic authors, and therefore merits inclusion in the framework. Tracy, in particular, underscored the incredible benefits he has experienced due to his self-advocacy:

> I want to tell you that my life experiences have been plentiful but really have included me making my own paths by seeking out ways on my own. The impact of learning to speak up and have a voice has been quite meaningful for me. I have typed life goals and dreams that have actually come true.

Opportunities to be involved in decision-making processes, especially regarding significant life choices and goals, were highly valued among other authors. Philip developed self-advocacy skills by advocating for his own inclusion in a general education curriculum. He explains that at his IEP meeting, "There were probably 10 people sitting around a big table. People smiled at me as I took my place at the head of the table with my iPad. Mom held my keyboard. Someone asked me, 'How could we help you the best?' I typed, 'Give me regular education.'" Similarly, in a fight to gain access to inclusion, Henry developed strong self-advocacy skills once he was given a chance to learn about "my access and education rights." In making his case to be included, he typed, "Today I read about Martin Luther King. The Civil Rights Act of 1964 granted equal rights to all people. I am a person. I want these rights. I want to go to school in my neighborhood. Why can't I?"

Including autistic students' voices in discussions that concern them and their education is highly recommended. Emma expressed an excellent suggestion to involve autistics in curriculum development: "Wouldn't it be great if autistic people's ideas were included in designing curriculum and the tests that are meant to evaluate them?" Absolutely! Larry effectively sums up his recommendation for educators and therapists: "For educators, I recommend teaching students the power of self-advocacy and speaking up to meet their goals in life." Table 8 presents a few examples from educators who provided opportunities for students to develop self-advocacy.

TABLE 8: EXAMPLES PROVIDING OPPORTUNITIES FOR SELF-ADVOCACY

Participant	Quote
Kristy (assistant teacher)	"I think the most important thing is really to work on shifting people's perspective and letting autistic people have the opportunity to explain what it's really like for them as opposed to everyone else saying what it is. That's something that we're really big on at Hirsch is advocating. We're constantly teaching our students how to advocate for themselves. The steps that they have to go through in order to make change and all of that. I think that a really important piece is teaching students about advocacy."

Participant	Quote
Tiffany (university disability resource center coordinator)	"'[Student's name], hey, I know we had developed this [student profile document to share with faculty]. This is something you would be okay with using?'" I'm respecting his decision and however he wants things facilitated [with his instructor]."

Concluding Remarks

The framework to support autistic students who spell and type to communicate provides a research-based roadmap for educators and therapists—from establishing foundational beliefs and practices to providing access to communication and, finally, to developing opportunities for student participation and engagement. Many of the concepts expressed in the framework have been established as good practices in the research literature. For instance, two research articles by Ashby & Kasa (2013) and Woodfield and Ashby (2016) confirmed that presuming competence, access to communication, and constructing opportunities for participation are critical supports to students who type to communicate. Both articles are highly recommended resources, particularly for those interested in learning about concrete strategies to construct opportunities for participation. The concepts presented in this chapter not only provide support and validation for past research findings, but are also organized into an overarching framework that can be used to inform the design of professional development for communication partners, educators, and therapists. This framework can be applied to supporting students who use all modes of augmentative and alternative communication and, therefore, should not be limited to students who learned to communicate using RPM and FC.

Historically, minimally speaking and nonspeaking autistic individuals have been excluded and marginalized. Their stories, shared in research studies and the media, have largely been told by people other than the autistic individuals themselves. Too often, narratives about people with autism perpetuate a deficit perspective, framing individuals with autism as damaged and incompetent individuals in need of fixing. *Communication Alternatives in Autism*—a book that places the narratives of autistic individuals with complex communication differences at center stage—is proof that times are changing. The narratives in the book indicate that individuals who use letter boards, keyboards, and other forms of augmentative and alternative communication are capable and deserving of intellectual engagement, contribution, and leadership. After all, access to communication is a civil right. In their resolution on the right to communicate, the organization, TASH, stated,

> People with communication disabilities must be allowed to use the communication system of their own choice in all communication interactions in any setting. In no case should an individual be left without a means to communicate. This includes all forms of augmentative and alternative communication, assistive technology, and access to a variety of effective methods and strategies. In any instances where such use is forbidden, there should be recourse to the legal and protective systems [TASH, 2016, para. 3].

The growing community of minimally speaking and nonspeaking students who demand communicative accommodations and inclusion in educational settings suggests that we are at a tipping point in history. Collectively, the authors—alongside a community of skilled communication partners, educators, friends, families, researchers, and allies—call for systemic change in providing equitable educational opportunities that will empower autistic individuals to flourish within the context of a life filled with dignity. This sort of change undeniably requires a transformation in belief systems and a commitment to change in policies and practices in schools and colleges. Such a monumental effort is imperative in the pursuit of justice, equity, and inclusion for all.

Appendix:
Examples of Approved Augmentative and Alternative Communication Accommodations by U.S. Schools That Have Enrolled Students Who Type and Spell to Communicate

*The following list of communication accommodations is not exhaustive. It does not include accommodations for sensory or motor needs, which are also important to support access to communication. Accommodations are presented in no particular order. Some items are repetitive or redundant but offer different ways to describe the same kinds of accommodations.

Access to electronic device to communicate at all times
Access to speech generating voice output device
Access to device with text-to-speech capabilities
Access to a wireless QWERTY keyboard.
Access to letter board.
Access to iPad with communication app.
Use of white board and markers for choice making
Access to alternative response options (choice board, short-cut boards, letter board, keyboard, alphabet stencils, math board, white board for selecting choices)
Access to stand for keyboard
Support of a trained communication partner who provides verbal, visual, and/or tactile support
Spell on letter board to communicate with trained 1:1 personal aide

Encourage use of tablet at all times to clarify responses

Extended time for response

Adult assistance including scribing and reading passages aloud

Support person may hold up communication tools (i.e., letter board, keyboard, iPad, calculator, etc.) during all class work and testing

Glossary

applied behavior analysis (ABA): The application of techniques on individuals with autism with the goal to change their observable behaviors. Families also refer to ABA as behavioral therapy.

apraxia: A medical diagnosis that indicates challenges with fine and gross motor planning needed to perform tasks or execute purposeful movements.

apraxia of speech: A type of apraxia that indicates difficulty with planning and coordinating movements to produce speech.

augmentative and alternative communication (AAC): Communication that supplements or replaces speech for those who experience challenges with speaking. Forms of AAC can include gestures, speech generating communication devices, communication boards with symbols or the alphabet, picture exchange communication systems, and more.

autism: A developmental disability often characterized by difficulties in communication and social interactions. Autistic individuals may experience issues with sensory processing, motor planning, and repetitive behaviors. While some people diagnosed with autism prefer person-first language (i.e., person with autism), others prefer identity-first language (i.e., autistic).

communication partner: An individual who supports the communication of autistics who use augmentative and alternative communication. Educational, emotional, and/or physical support may be provided while the communicator learns, develops, and produces communicative output. A communication partner is also known as facilitator in the realm of facilitated communication.

disability rights: A movement largely led by disabled individuals to achieve equal human rights. While disability rights can focus on striving for equal opportunities to access buildings, housing, and employment, many of the references to disability rights in this book center on communication rights, or the opportunity to access and choose their mode of communication.

facilitated communication (FC): A method of communication used by non-speaking and minimally speaking individuals who are physically supported by a facilitator to type, point, or spell to communicate. Physical support from the facilitator is meant to be faded over time—from the hand, wrist, arm, shoulder, and the back—as the communicator becomes more independent. FC is also known as supported typing.

inclusion: When students with disabilities are placed in age-appropriate general education settings with their non-disabled peers. The opposite of inclusion involves placing students with disabilities in segregated or restricted educational environments with little to no access to an age-appropriate curriculum and nondisabled peers.

keyboard: A panel of keys with the alphabet and other symbols to operate a communication device. Usually keyboards are connected wirelessly to tablets with communication apps and speech-generating capabilities.

letter board: A laminated board that features the alphabet and, in some cases, punctuation or commonly used words. In many cases, the communication partner holds the letter board as the communicator points to letters and symbols printed on the board to generate words or statements. Letter boards are referred to as alphabet boards by some.

nonspeaking: The absence of speech. This term evolved from the word nonverbal, which suggests deficits in receptive and expressive language in addition to challenges in speech. The term nonspeaking does not suggest intellectual disability, but focuses on lack of speech alone.

rapid prompting method (RPM): An educational method created by Soma Mukhopadhyay, founder of Helping Autism through Learning and Outreach organization, that leads to communication for nonspeaking and minimally speaking individuals. The communicator points to letters on a stencil, letter board, or keyboard to spell words and statements.

reinforcer: Objects or actions that are used to increase the incidence or occurrence of a particular behavior. Reinforcers may be tangible (e.g., candy, toys, community outings) or intangible (e.g., verbal praise, high-fives). Reinforcers are a critical component of applied behavioral analysis in the shaping of an individual's behaviors.

stencil (also known as an alphabet stencil or letter board stencil): A hard plastic board with the alphabet cut out of it. Communicators point with their finger or a pencil to each letter to generate words or statements.

stimming (also known as self-stimulation or self-stimulatory behaviors): Repetitive movements, use of objects, or speech that, for some individuals, can interfere with learning or performing daily activities. Individuals engage in stimming for a variety of reasons, including to self-regulate, provide sensory input, block out sensory input, manage pain, and manage emotions.

RPM and FC Resources

Books

Anatomy of Autism: A Pocket Guide for Educators, Parents, and Students
  Diego M. Peña (2017)

Autism and the Myth of the Person Alone
  Douglas Biklen (2005)

Autism: Sensory-Movement Differences and Diversity
  Martha R. Leary & Anne M. Donnellan (2014)

Carly's Voice: Breaking Through Autism
  Arthur Fleischmann & Carly Fleischmann (2012)

Fall Down 7 Times Get Up 8: A Young Man's Voice from the Silence of Autism
  Naoki Higashida (2017)

How Can I Talk If My Lips Don't Move? Inside My Autistic Mind
  Tito Mukhopadhyay (2008)

Ido in Autismland: Climbing Out of Autism's Silent Prison
  Ido Kedar (2012)

Plankton Dreams: What I Learned in Special Ed
  Tito Mukhopadhyay (2015)

The Reason I Jump: The Inner Voice of a Thirteen Year Old Boy with Autism
  Naoki Higashida (2013)

Typed Words, Loud Voices
  Amy Sequenzia & Elizabeth J. Grace (2015)

Documentaries

Autism Is a World (2004)
A Mother's Courage: Talking Back to Autism (2010)
Deej (2017)

Dillan's Path (2016)

Dillan's Voice (2016)

My Classic Life as an Artist: A Portrait of Larry Bissonnette (2005)

My Voice: One Man's Journey Through the Silent World of Autism (2017)

Spectrum: A Story of the Mind (2017)

The Power of Finding Your Voice (Tedx Talk by Parisa Khosravi) (2017)

Unspoken (2017)

Wretches and Jabberers (2010)

Organizations

A.C.E. Teaching and Consulting

Autism and Communication Center, California Lutheran University

Autistic Self-Advocacy Network (ASAN)

Connections School of Atlanta

Everyone Communicates

Golden Hat Foundation

Growing Kids Therapy Center

Helping Autism through Learning and Outreach (HALO)

Hirsch Academy

Hope, Expression and Education for Individuals with Severe Disabilities (HEED)

Hussman Institute for Autism

Institute on Communication and Inclusion, Syracuse University

Invictus Academy Tampa Bay

Nonspeaking Community Consortium

Olliebean

Open Mind School

Optimal Rhythms/Access Academy

Reach Every Voice

Resource for Education, Advocacy, Communication, and Housing (REACH)

RPM+ for Autism and Other Disabilities

TASH

United for Communication Choice

Unlocking Voices—Using RPM

Wellspring Guild

References

American Speech-Language Hearing Association (2018). *ASHA supports effective services leading to independent communication.* Retrieved from https://www.asha.org/Independent-Communication/

Ashby, C. & Kasa, C. (2013). Pointing forward: Supporting academic access for individuals that type to communicate. *ASHA Perspectives on Augmentative and Alternative Communication, 22*(3), 143–156.

Ashby, C., Woodfield, C., & Delia, Q. (2016). Communication is the root of necessity: Constructing communicative competence. In C. Ashby & M. Cosier (Eds.), *Enacting change from within: Disability studies meets teaching and teacher education.* New York, NY: Peter Lang.

Autistic Self-Advocacy Network (n.d.). *About our mission.* Retrieved from http://autisticadvocacy.org/about-asan/

Bal, V.H., Katz T., Bishop S, & Krasileva K. (2016). Understanding definitions of minimally verbal across instruments: Evidence for subgroups within minimally verbal children and adolescents with autism spectrum disorder. *Journal of Child Psychology and Psychiatry, 57*(12), 1424–1433.

Belnavis, D. (2018, June 25). *An open letter to ASHA advocating for the right to a communication method of choice.* Retrieved from https://juniperhill-farms.org, 2018.

Bigozzi, L., Zanobini, M., Tarchi, C., Cozzani, F., & Camba, R. (2012). Facilitated communication and autistic children: The problem of authorship. *Life Span and Disability, 15*, 55–74.

Biklen, D., & Burke, J. (2006). Presuming competence. *Equity & Excellence in Education, 39*, 166–175.

Blischak, D.M., Lombardino, L.J., & Dyson, A.T. (2003). Use of speech-generating devices: In support of natural speech. *Augmentative and Alternative Communication, 19*(1), 29–35.

Botash, A.S., Babuts, D., Mitchell, N., O'Hara, M., Lynch, L., & Manuel, J. (1994). Evaluations of children who have disclosed sexual abuse via facilitated communication. *Archives of Pediatric and Adolescent Medicine, 148*, 1282–1287.

Cardinal, D.N., & M.A. Falvey. (2014). The Maturing of Facilitated Communication A Means Toward Independent Communication. *Research and Practice for Persons with Severe Disabilities, 39*(3), 189–194.

Cattaneo, L., Fabbri-Destro, M., Boria, S., Pieraccini, C., Monti, A., Cossu, G., & Rizzolatti, G. (2007). Impairment of actions chains in autism and its possible role in intention understanding. *Proceedings of the National Academy of Sciences, 104,* 17825–17830.

Courchesne, V., Meilleur, A.S., Poulin-Lord, M.P., Dawson, M., & Soulières, I. (2015). Autistic children at risk of being underestimated: School-based pilot study of a strength-informed assessment. *Molecular Autism, 6*(12), 1–10.

Deacy, E., Jennings, F., & O'Halloran, A. (2016). Rapid prompting method (RPM): A suitable intervention for students with ASD? *REACH Journal of Special Needs Education in Ireland, 29*(2), 92–100.

Developmental Disability Services Division of Vermont (2018). *Guidelines for handling allegations of abuse while using facilitated communication.* Retrieved from https://ddsd.vermont.gov/sites/ddsd/files/documents/ Guidelines_for_Allegations_of_Abuse_FC.pdf

Donnellan, A. (1984). The criterion of the least dangerous assumption. *Behavioral Disorders, 9*(2), 141–150.

Donnellan, A., Hill, D., & Leary, M. (2010). Rethinking autism: Implications of sensory and movement differences. *Disability Studies Quarterly,* 30(1), 1–26.

Donnellan, A., Hill, D., & Leary, M. (2013). Rethinking autism: Implications of sensory and movement differences for understanding and support. *Frontiers in Integrative Neuroscience, 6*(124), 1–11.

Donnellan, A., Leary, M., & Robledo, J. (2006). "I can't get started": Stress and the role of movement differences for individuals with the autism label. In G. Baron, J. Groden, G. Groden, & L. Lipsitt (Eds.), *Stress and Coping in Autism* (pp. 205–245). Oxford: Oxford University Press.

Duncan, A. (2010). *Fulfilling the promise of IDEA: Remarks on the 35th anniversary of the Individuals with Disabilities Education Act.* Retrieved from https://www.ed.gov/news/speeches/fulfilling-promise-idea-remarks-35th-anniversary-individuals-disabilities-education-act

Green, D., Charman, T., Pickles, A., Chandler, S., Loucas, T., Simonoff, E., & Baird, G. (2009). Impairment in movement skills of children with autistic spectrum disorders. *Developmental Medicine & Child Neurology, 51,* 311–316.

Kedar, I. (2011). *Ido Kedar speech at Los Angeles Autism Walk Now.* Retrieved from https://autismspeaksblog.wordpress.com/2011/04/26/ido-kedar-speech/.

Kedar, I. (2012). *Ido in Autismland.* Woodland Hills, CA: Sharon Kedar.

McQuiddy, V., & Brennan, A.M. (2016). Occupational therapy using Rapid Prompting Method: A case report. *Autism Open Access* 6(1), 1–4.

Millar, D.C., Light, J.C., & Schlosser, R.W. (2006). The impact of augmentative and alternative communication intervention on the speech production of individuals with developmental disabilities: A research review. *Journal of Speech, Language, and Hearing Research, 49,* 248–264.

Mirenda, P. (2008). A back door approach to autism and AAC. *Augmentative and Alternative Communication 24*: 220–234.

National Research Council (2001). *Educating Children with Autism.* Washington, D.C.: National Academy Press.

Peña, D.M. (2017). *Anatomy of Autism.* Camarillo, CA: Create Space.

Rossetti, Z.S., Cheng, P., & Lavoy, H. (2012). Practicing message passing skills. *Institute for Communication and Inclusion Newsletter* (1), 3–7.

Stanton-Salazar, R. (1997). A social capital framework for understanding the socialization of racial minority children and youths. *Harvard Educational Review, 67*(1), 1–41.

TASH (2016). *TASH resolution on the right to communicate.* Retrieved from https://tash.org/about/resolutions/tash-resolution-right-communicate-2016/

Thurlow, M. L., Quenemoen, R.F., Lazarus, S.S. (2011). *Meeting the needs of special education students: Recommendations for the Race to the Top consortia and states.* Washington, D.C.: Arabella Advisors.

U.S. Department of Education (2016). *Parent and educator resource guide to Section 504 in public elementary and secondary schools.* Retrieved from https://www2.ed.gov/about/offices/list/ocr/docs/504-resource-guide-201612.pdf

Woodfield, C. & Ashby, C. (2016). "The right path of equality": Supporting high school students with autism who type to communicate. *International Journal of Inclusive Education, 20*(4) 1–20.

Index